Biodiversity and Development Finance 2015-2022

CONTRIBUTING TO TARGET 19
OF THE KUNMING-MONTREAL GLOBAL
BIODIVERSITY FRAMEWORK

OECD
BETTER POLICIES FOR BETTER LIVES

Please cite this publication as:
OECD (2024), *Biodiversity and Development Finance 2015-2022: Contributing to Target 19 of the Kunming-Montreal Global Biodiversity Framework*, OECD Publishing, Paris, https://doi.org/10.1787/d26526ad-en.

ISBN 978-92-64-43788-3 (print)
ISBN 978-92-64-70885-3 (PDF)
ISBN 978-92-64-98321-2 (HTML)
ISBN 978-92-64-57774-9 (epub)

Revised version, October 2024
Details of revisions available at: https://www.oecd.org/en/publications/support/corrigenda.html

Photo credits: Cover © jacquesvandinteren/Getty Images.

Corrigenda to OECD publications may be found at: https://www.oecd.org/en/publications/support/corrigenda.html.

Foreword

A new era for biodiversity was ushered in when Parties agreed to the United Nations Convention on Biological Diversity's (CBD) Kunming-Montreal Global Biodiversity Framework (KMGBF) in December 2022. The KMGBF includes new, and ambitious, resource mobilisation provisions (Goal D and Target 19), notably aiming to increase the level of financial resources from all sources to at least USD 200 billion per year by 2030, including via international public resources for biodiversity by at least USD 20 billion per year by 2025 and to at least USD 30 billion per year by 2030 (target 19a).

The OECD report *A Decade of Development Finance for Biodiversity*, released in 2023, analysed the contribution of development finance for biodiversity in the period 2011-20, which coincides with the implementation period of the CBD Strategic Plan on Biodiversity and its Aichi Targets – the roadmap driving international development co-operation action for biodiversity over that decade. In particular, it also showed that the members of the OECD Development Assistance Committee (DAC) that are Parties to the CBD collectively achieved the Aichi Target 20 that referred to development finance.

Building on the methodology and data developed in *A Decade of Development Finance for Biodiversity*, the OECD initiated an annual report series on biodiversity and development finance with the aim to track the contribution of development finance towards Target 19 of the KMGBF. As such, and as part of this series, the present report provides an overview of trends in biodiversity-related development finance from 2015 to 2022 from a range of sources – namely, bilateral DAC members and other bilateral providers including South-South and triangular co-operation, multilateral development banks and other multilateral institutions, private philanthropies, and private finance mobilised by public development finance.

While KMGBF Target 19 encompasses both public and private international flows for biodiversity allocated to developing countries, the data collected by the OECD-DAC *Creditor Reporting System* takes a development finance angle, and mainly focuses on public international flows, but also includes private philanthropy flows and private finance mobilised by public development finance. In addition, the report provides insights into biodiversity-related international development finance themes such as the interplay of biodiversity with climate change, gender equality, and Indigenous peoples and local communities.

Acknowledgements

This report was prepared by Dominique Blaquier and Juan Casado-Asensio. It was produced under the supervision of Jens Sedemund, with guidance from Frederik Matthys and overall leadership of María del Pilar Garrido Gonzalo. It benefited from the inputs of several OECD colleagues: Wiebke Bartz-Zuccala, Cibele Cesca, Abdoulaye Fabregas, Tomáš Hos, Fatoumata Ngom, Nadine Piefer-Söyler and Cécile Sangaré (Development Co-operation Directorate); Katia Karousakis and Edward Perry (Environment Directorate); Bridget Donovan and Jose Enrique Garcilazo (Centre for Entrepreneurship, SMEs, Regions and Cities); as well as Marisa Berbegal-Ibañez and Camilo Gamba (International Forum on Total Official Support for Sustainable Development). In addition, the authors would like to thank Sokob Challener for administrative support, as well as Stephanie Coic, Karena Garnier, Ola Kasneci and Henri-Bernard Solignac-Lecomte for communications, Jennifer Allain for copy editing and Simon Biermann for French translations support.

The report was conceptualised with, and received steering and useful comments from members of the Development Assistance Committee (DAC), the Environment and Development Co-operation Network (ENVIRONET) and its Friends of Biodiversity Group, namely: Dirk Platzen (Australian Department of Foreign Affairs and Trade); Sandra Wibmer (Austrian Development Agency); Catherine Potvin, Tiffanie Rainville, Maude St-Onge and Michelle Tremblay (Global Affairs Canada); Juliane Muellner (European Commission Directorate-General for Environment); Aurelie Godefroy and Hugo-Maria Schally (European Commission Directorate-General for International Partnerships); Stéphane Cieniewski and Julien Velud (French Treasury); Adrien Bolgert (French Ministry for Europe and Foreign Affairs); Jean-Noël Roulleau (French Development Agency); Florian Doerr, Sylvia Reinhardt and David Weihrauch (German Agency for International Co-operation); Johannes Haas, Claudia Hiepe, Michael Lehmann and Sören Müller (German Ministry for Economic Co-operation and Development); Robert Sheridan (Irish Department of Foreign Affairs); Lorenzo Orioli and Iacopo Sinibaldi (Italian Agency for Development Co-operation); Filippo Lonardo, Adolfo Morrone, Silvia Maria Lucia Santangelo, Francesco Serpi and Alessia Tassinari (Italian Ministry of Foreign Affairs and International Co-operation); Ivo Walsmit (Dutch Ministry of Foreign Affairs); Andrea Stewart (New Zealand Ministry of Foreign Affairs and Trade); Ida Hellmark, Hilde Dahl, Geir Erichsrud and Thea Namtvedt Tuv (Norwegian Agency for Development Co-operation); Miguel Galante (Camões Cooperation and Language Institute, Portuguese Ministry of Foreign Affairs); Anna Åxelsson (Swedish International Development Cooperation Agency); Michaela Wenner (Swiss Agency for Development and Co-operation); Lucretia Landmann (Swiss Federal Office for the Environment); Luke Bailey (UK Foreign, Commonwealth and Development Office); Jessica Bridgman, Nicholas Bruschi and Emma Jones (UK Department for Environment, Food and Rural Affairs); Alice Caravani (UK Department of Energy Security and Net Zero).

Additional inputs were provided by Katy Scholfield (Arcus Foundation); Birgitte Feiring (Charapa); Casey Box (Christensen Fund); Joko Arif (David and Lucile Packard Foundation); Adonai Herrera-Martinez (EBRD on behalf of the MDBs' Nature Working Group); Claire Taylor (Ford Foundation); Lourdes Inga and Anabel López (International Funders for Indigenous Peoples); Joan Carling (Indigenous People's Rights International); Katherine Despot-Belmonte (UNEP-WCMC); and Alejandro Kilpatrick (UNFCCC).

Table of contents

FIGURES

TABLES

Abbreviations and acronyms

CBD	Convention on Biological Diversity
COP	Conference of the Parties
CRS	Creditor Reporting System
DAC	Development Assistance Committee
DFC	Development Finance Corporation
DFCD	Dutch Fund for Climate and Development
DNS	Dept for nature swap
EU	European Union
GCF	Green Climate Fund
GEF	Global Environment Facility
GIZ	German Agency for International Co-operation *Deutsche Gesellschaft für Internationale Zusammenarbeit*
GFFP	Global Forest Finance Pledge
GPA	Gender Plan of Action
IDB	Inter-American Development Bank
IFAD	International Fund for Agricultural Development
IFC	International Finance Corporation
IPs and LCs	Indigenous peoples and local communities
KMGBF	Kunming-Montreal Global Biodiversity Framework
LAC	Latin America and the Caribbean
LDC	Least developed country
LIC	Low-income country
LMICs	Lower middle-income countries and territories
MDB	Multilateral development bank
MIC	Middle-income country
MINBUZA	Dutch Ministry of Foreign Affairs
NbS	Nature-based solution

NBSAP	National Biodiversity Strategy and Action Plan
NGO	Non-governmental organisation
ODA	Official development assistance
ODF	Official development finance
OOF	Other official flows
PSI	Private sector instrument
SDG	Sustainable Development Goal
SIDS	Small island developing state
South-South	South-South and triangular co-operation
TOSSD	Total official support for sustainable development
UMICs	Upper middle-income countries and territories
UN	United Nations
UNCCD	United Nations Convention to Combat Desertification
UNPFII	United Nations Permanent Forum on Indigenous Issues
USAID	United States Agency for International Development
USD	United States Dollar

Executive summary

Development finance for biodiversity: Trends over 2015-22

- Official development finance (ODF) for biodiversity increased from all sources between 2015 and 2022.
- Overall, the total increased sharply over this period considering two approaches that either:
  - apply a 40% coefficient on a portion of data as having a *significant* objective (i.e. biodiversity-specific ODF), ranging from USD 7.3 billion in 2015 to USD 11.1 billion in 2021 and USD 15.4 billion in 2022; or
  - reflect the full values of these flows (i.e. biodiversity-related ODF), ranging from USD 10.9 billion in 2015 to USD 18.5 billion in 2021 and USD 25.8 billion in 2022.
- All in all, the contribution of development finance to the Kunming-Montreal Global Biodiversity Framework (KMGBF) is currently 23% away from its Target 19a (i.e. USD 20 billion by 2025), considering the biodiversity-specific approach.
- From 2015 to 2022, bilateral Development Assistance Committee (DAC) members' ODF for biodiversity grew between 8%-27%. However, flows towards biodiversity as a *principal* objective decreased by 17%, from USD 4.6 billion in 2015 to USD 3.2 billion in 2021 and USD 3.8 billion in 2022. Furthermore, biodiversity considerations still represent a relatively low share of the total ODF portfolio (4%-7%, or USD 6.1-9.7 billion on average over the period). While mainstreaming across activities is essential – and particularly in nature-dependent sectors – donors may consider raising their efforts towards core biodiversity-related activities, to increase and improve biodiversity and its ecosystem services and ensure that their impacts are sustained in time.
- Estimates of multilateral institutions' ODF for biodiversity grew between 716%-824% over the period. Contrary to bilateral ODF, contributions to activities with *principal* biodiversity objectives under the Rio marker system have been increasing, from USD 0.1 billion in 2015 to USD 1.1 billion in 2021 and USD 2.1 billion in 2022. However, the share of biodiversity-related activities out of the total multilateral ODF portfolio remained relatively low (2%-3%, or USD 2.4-4.8 billion on average over the period) and need to increase for these institutions to contribute meaningfully to the KMGBF.
- While bilateral non-DAC providers – including South-South and triangular co-operation – provide relatively low and volatile levels of international finance (e.g. fluctuating from USD 40.2 million in 2018 to USD 26.9 million in 2021 and USD 30 million in 2022), their engagement in biodiversity issues has been growing.
- Biodiversity-related development finance from private philanthropies increased from USD 501 million in 2017 to USD 700 million in 2022, yet it decreased compared to 2021 (USD 1 billion).
- Private finance mobilised with public finance has more than doubled, from USD 748 million in 2021 to USD 1.8 billion in 2022. However, these amounts are still far from those achieved in other policy areas, such as climate change (USD 16.1 billion on average over 2017-22), and meeting Target 19 of the KMGBF requires greater mobilisation of private flows.

Allocations by financial instrument, income level and region

- While DAC members' support to biodiversity was mainly delivered in the form of grants, multilateral institutions primarily used concessional loans – in line with their respective mandates. Notably, the bulk of multilateral financing is attributed to multilateral development banks, accounting for 71% of the total over 2015-22. In contrast, DAC donors mainly provide official development assistance, which is, by definition, concessional in character, comprising grants and soft loans.
- Least-developed countries and low-income countries mainly received grants from both types of providers (83% of DAC members' ODF over 2015-22 vs. 52% of multilateral finance). Middle-income countries mainly received concessional loans from these providers (53% and 84%, respectively).
- Overall, Africa and Asia were the regions that benefited the most from DAC members, receiving USD 2.9 billion (39% of total biodiversity-related ODF) and USD 2 billion (27%), respectively, on average annually over the period. Asia was the first destination of multilateral institutions, receiving 39% of biodiversity-related finance, followed by America (34%) and Africa (25%).

Sectoral distribution

- Over 2015-22, biodiversity-related ODF from DAC members and multilateral institutions concentrated in activities related to general environment protection, agriculture and water. However, the degree to which biodiversity was integrated across sectors varied among providers. DAC members mainstreamed biodiversity in 23% of their development finance for agriculture while it was 12% for multilateral institutions. In water-related activities, these percentages were 20% and 7%, respectively, and for energy 3% and less than 1%, respectively. In forestry there was a substantial integration of biodiversity concerns (78% for DAC members and 64% for multilateral institutions). Nevertheless, the variable integration of biodiversity-related considerations across sectors highlights the need for greater and more comprehensive biodiversity mainstreaming.

Thematic analysis: Climate change, gender equality, Indigenous peoples and local communities

- The share of biodiversity-related ODF that also addresses climate change has steadily increased, from 78% in 2015 to 92% in 2022. However, the opposite does not hold true, as biodiversity objectives are only reflected in 20% of total climate-related ODF on average over the same period, a trend that declined from 24% in 2015 to 19% in 2022. Given that total volumes towards climate-related objectives are at least three times higher than towards biodiversity, and as momentum to reach the Paris Agreement continues increasing, providers must integrate biodiversity-related considerations in climate programming, to maximise co-benefits and address trade-offs.
- The share of biodiversity-related ODF addressing gender equality increased from 46% in 2015 to 68% in 2022. Yet only about 12% of development finance targeting gender equality also included biodiversity in 2021 and 2022. DAC members could explore integrating biodiversity and gender equality across their portfolios, acknowledging women's role in conserving and sustainably using biodiversity, including their involvement in policy making and implementation.
- The estimated share of biodiversity-related ODF targeting Indigenous peoples and local communities (IPs and LCs) remains low, representing 6% of DAC members' total biodiversity-related ODF in 2022, in line with past assessments. Most of this funding (56%) corresponds to activities addressing the Convention on Biological Diversity's objectives as a main priority, underscoring the connections between IPs and LCs and nature.

1 The importance of development finance to achieve Target 19 of the Kunming-Montreal Global Biodiversity Framework

At the 15th Conference of the Parties (COP15) of the United Nations Convention on Biological Diversity (CBD) in 2022, Parties agreed to the Kunming-Montreal Global Biodiversity Framework (KMGBF). Target 19 of the KMGBF commits developed countries[1] (and other countries that voluntarily assume obligations of developed country Parties) to a collective goal of mobilising at least USD 20 billion per year by 2025, and at least USD 30 billion per year by 2030, from all international sources, for biodiversity-related action in developing countries, in particular the least developed countries and small island developing States, as well as countries with economies in transition. Official development finance (ODF) is one of the means of accomplishing this (see Box 1.1).

Box 1.1. Finance provisions of the Kunming-Montreal Global Biodiversity Framework

The Kunming-Montreal Global Biodiversity Framework (KMGBF) includes a set of four global goals for 2050 (CBD, 2022[1]). Goal D is pertinent to development finance: "Adequate means of implementation, including financial resources, capacity-building, technical and scientific co-operation, and access to and transfer of technology to fully implement the Kunming-Montreal Global Biodiversity Framework are secured and equitably accessible to all Parties, especially developing countries, in particular the least developed countries and small island developing States, as well as countries with economies in transition, progressively closing the biodiversity finance gap of USD 700 billion per year, and aligning financial flows with the Kunming-Montreal Global Biodiversity Framework and the 2050 Vision for biodiversity."

The KMGBF also covers 23 action-oriented targets to be achieved by 2030. Under Target 19 Parties agreed to: "Substantially and progressively increase the level of financial resources from all sources, in an effective, timely and easily accessible manner, including domestic, international, public and private resources, in accordance with Article 20 of the Convention, to implement national biodiversity strategies and action plans, by 2030 mobilising at least USD 200 billion per year, including by:

a) Increasing total biodiversity-related international financial resources from developed countries, including official development assistance, and from countries that voluntarily assume obligations of developed country Parties, to developing countries, in particular the least developed countries and small island developing states, as well as countries with economies in transition, to at least USD 20 billion per year by 2025, and to at least USD 30 billion per year by 2030;

b) Significantly increasing domestic resource mobilisation, facilitated by the preparation and implementation of national biodiversity finance plans or similar instruments according to national needs, priorities and circumstances;

c) Leveraging private finance, promoting blended finance, implementing strategies for raising new and additional resources, and encouraging the private sector to invest in biodiversity, including through impact funds and other instruments;

d) Stimulating innovative schemes such as payment for ecosystem services, green bonds, biodiversity offsets and credits, benefit-sharing mechanisms, with environmental and social safeguards;

e) Optimising co-benefits and synergies of finance targeting the biodiversity and climate crises;

f) Enhancing the role of collective actions, including by indigenous peoples and local communities, Mother Earth centric actions and non-market-based approaches including community based natural resource management and civil society cooperation and solidarity aimed at the conservation of biodiversity; and

g) Enhancing the effectiveness, efficiency and transparency of resource provision and use."

Progress towards Target 19 would also be supported by other finance-related KMGBF Targets, mainly: Target 14 on mainstreaming and alignment of financial flows; Target 15 on business assessment, disclosure and reduction of biodiversity-related risks and impacts; and Target 18 on reducing harmful subsidies and scaling up positive incentives. In addition, COP15 also approved the Monitoring Framework for the KMGBF (CBD, 2022[2]), including the headline indicators and the online reporting tool and global review, as the way of measuring progress on the implementation of KMGBF Goals and Targets, and a Resource Mobilisation Strategy (CBD, 2022[3]).

ODF is mainly tracked by the OECD through its *Creditor Reporting System* (CRS). Since 1998, the OECD Development Assistance Committee (DAC) has monitored development finance targeting the objectives of the Rio Conventions, including the CBD, through four "Rio markers" (biodiversity, desertification, climate change mitigation and adaptation). Countries and institutions reporting their ODF to the OECD signal flows to biodiversity-related activities using the biodiversity Rio marker, as well as through two Sustainable Development Goal (SDG) tags – SDG 14 (marine biodiversity) and SDG 15 (terrestrial biodiversity). These data are reported by a range of stakeholders, namely: bilateral DAC members; bilateral providers beyond the DAC, including South-South and triangular co-operation providers (hereafter "South-South providers"); multilateral development banks and other multilateral institutions; private philanthropic foundations; and private finance mobilised by public development finance.

Using these data, the OECD initiated an annual report series on Biodiversity and Development Finance (OECD, 2023[4]) with the aim to track the contribution of development finance towards Target 19 of the KMGBF. As such, and as part of this series, the present report provides an overview of trends in biodiversity-related development finance from 2015 to 2022, updating previous OECD work in this area, notably OECD (2023[5]) and Casado-Asensio, Blaquier and Sedemund (2022[6]), which analyse the contribution of development finance for biodiversity for the decade 2011-20, coinciding with the implementation period of the CBD Strategic Plan on Biodiversity and its Aichi Targets. It also provides an update of the relevant sections of *A Comprehensive Overview of Global Biodiversity Finance* report, which provides an aggregate estimate of global biodiversity finance, covering public, private, domestic and international finance (OECD, 2020[7]).

The present report is based on a comprehensive methodology developed to identify biodiversity-related activities in the OECD-DAC CRS and *Total Official Support for Sustainable Development* (TOSSD) databases (see Annex A). Biodiversity-related development finance refers to official development assistance (ODA) and other official flows (OOF) that contribute to the conservation, restoration and sustainable use of biodiversity.

Annual updates of biodiversity-related development finance can help track the implementation of the resource mobilisation provisions of the KMGBF with the range of development finance sources currently captured by the OECD and the International Forum on TOSSD (i.e. the CRS and TOSSD, respectively). Shedding light on these flows can help DAC members, other providers of development co-operation, civil society, partner countries and other stakeholders as they embark in their preparations for the 16th COP of the CBD in Cali, Colombia; discussions on biodiversity and nature at the 29th meeting of the United Nations Framework Convention on Climate Change (UNFCCC) COP in Baku, Azerbaijan; and at the 16th United Nations Convention to Combat Desertification (UNCCD) COP in Riyadh, Saudi Arabia. More generally, the report also provides relevant inputs to monitor the implementation of the *OECD DAC Declaration on a New Approach to Align Development Co-operation with the Goals of the Paris Agreement on Climate Change* (OECD, 2021[8]).

Total biodiversity-related international finance from developed countries, or countries that voluntarily assume obligations of developed countries, to developing countries includes both international public and private sector financial resources. Regarding international private sector finance allocated to developing countries, this report captures finance from private philanthropy and private finance mobilised by bilateral and multilateral public finance, as included in the OECD-DAC CRS. However, biodiversity-related international finance could also encompass other sources of international private finance flows (e.g. flows from civil society, the private sector or high-net-worth individuals) that could be considered international development finance but that are not captured in this report. For a comprehensive overview of global biodiversity finance covering public, private, domestic and international finance, see OECD (2020[7]).

In addition, enhanced statistical reporting can help better capture biodiversity flows even from stakeholders already reporting to both the CRS and TOSSD (Box 1.2). Other aspects of Target 19 of the KMGBF also fall within the remit of development co-operation (see Box 1.1) yet are not readily quantifiable with specific targets or indicators. Hence, this report also presents data contributing to: Target 19(b) looking into examples of development finance that support enabling environments and policy support; Target 19(e) looking at trends between development finance targeting biodiversity and climate change objectives; Target 19(f) looking into biodiversity-related development finance related to Indigenous peoples and local communities; as well as other relevant analysis including development finance targeting both biodiversity and gender equality objectives.

Compared to the 2023 report, this report provides the following novelties:

- Greater coverage of bilateral development finance from OECD-DAC members, including a breakdown by DAC member, and by looking at biodiversity-related development finance addressing multiple issues (e.g. climate change, gender equality, Indigenous peoples and local communities), as well as examples to strengthen enabling environments and local capacities to support domestic resource mobilisation.
- Greater insights of bilateral development finance beyond the DAC, including South-South and triangular co-operation (through trends on regional allocations, channels of delivery, sectoral breakdowns and examples).
- Greater identification of biodiversity-related development finance by multilateral development banks and other multilateral institutions reporting to the OECD-DAC CRS.
- Greater coverage of private philanthropies, including a breakdown of philanthropic providers, and insights on additional private philanthropies and the opportunities to increase reporting.

- Greater coverage of mobilised private finance, looking into leveraging mechanisms, allocations by regions and level of income, and highlighting the importance of the private sector as a key partner to advance the international development agenda.

For further information, see methodology in Annex A.

Box 1.2. Stock take report to improve biodiversity-related development finance statistics

The biodiversity Rio marker helps track the mainstreaming of biodiversity objectives across development finance portfolios and is often used by Development Assistance Committee (DAC) members to report on their financial commitments to the CBD. Recognising the need to improve the reporting on biodiversity-related development finance, members agreed in 2024 to update the DAC statistical framework on biodiversity (i.e. biodiversity Rio marker) by strengthening data transparency, availability and coherence.

Drawing from a survey launched in January 2024 as well as on evidence from a review of DAC statistics and desk research, the OECD produced a stock take report on members' biodiversity-related reporting practices (Casado-Asensio, Blaquier and Gualberti, 2024[9]), which sought to identify possible constraints and opportunities for refining data collection on biodiversity-related development finance. Survey responses were received from all 32 DAC members. Several conclusions can be drawn from the stock take, which can help improve the application of the biodiversity Rio marker and in reporting to the OECD-DAC CRS (and, where applicable, to the CBD):

- Members have come a long way in screening their ODA and other official flows activities against the biodiversity Rio marker, but further efforts could be deployed. The approval of the reporting methods for "private sector instruments", can be an opportunity to ensure greater biodiversity-related screening.
- Further training and guidance materials are needed for expert and non-expert policy officers (across the whole system, both in headquarters and in the field) and for statistical reporters to better use the marker, providing clarity and consistency in the assignment of the marker, as well as enhancing comparability across members.
- Additional review and quality assurance tools (notably exploring artificial intelligence) could alleviate the reporting burden on biodiversity, improve data quality and provide solutions when capacity is limited. These tools could also be used, as needed, for retro marketing data.
- For members without a dedicated biodiversity-related development finance portfolio, engaging in the update of the Rio marker on biodiversity can help tease out biodiversity-related activities, e.g. in their environment or climate change portfolios, as indeed the marker can help promote and track mainstreaming.
- Guidance is also needed on how to apply the biodiversity and other Rio markers coherently, as well as using the environment marker and the Sustainable Development Goals.

DAC members are currently working to update and develop guidance on the biodiversity Rio marker, notably to align with the Kunming-Montreal Global Biodiversity Framework (KMGBF), including to improve the reporting directives (e.g. definition, eligibility criteria, indicative table) and to continue raising awareness on the importance of biodiversity-related development finance overall (e.g. through annual reports tracking the contribution of development finance to the KMGBF).

Source: (Casado-Asensio, Blaquier and Gualberti, 2024[9])

References

Casado-Asensio, J., D. Blaquier and G. Gualberti (2024), "Stock Take Report on Members' Reporting Practices on Biodiversity-related Development Finance and Reporting against International Obligations", *DCD/DAC/ENV(2024)1/REV1/FINAL*, https://one.oecd.org/document/DCD/DAC/ENV(2024)1/REV1/FINAL/en/pdf. [9]

Casado-Asensio, J., D. Blaquier and J. Sedemund (2022), "Biodiversity and development finance: Main trends, 2011-20", *OECD Development Co-operation Working Papers*, No. 110, OECD Publishing, Paris, https://doi.org/10.1787/b04b14b7-en. [6]

CBD (2022), *Kunming-Montreal Global Biodiversity Framework*, https://www.cbd.int/doc/c/e6d3/cd1d/daf663719a03902a9b116c34/cop-15-l-25-en.pdf (accessed on 15 July 2024). [1]

CBD (2022), *Resource Mobilization*, https://www.cbd.int/doc/c/22fb/be2c/02e31154c4d4429de03caefe/cop-15-l-29-en.pdf (accessed on 15 July 2024). [3]

CBD (2006), *Guidance to the financial mechanism*, https://www.cbd.int/doc/decisions/cop-08/cop-08-dec-18-en.pdf (accessed on 9 July 2024). [10]

CBD/COP/DEC/15/5 (ed.) (2022), *Decision adopted by the conference of the parties to the convention on biological diversity: 15/5. Monitoring framework for the kunming-montreal global biodiversity framework*, https://www.cbd.int/doc/decisions/cop-15/cop-15-dec-05-en.pdf (accessed on 3 April 2024). [2]

OECD (2023), *A Decade of Development Finance for Biodiversity*, OECD Publishing, Paris, https://doi.org/10.1787/e6c182aa-en. [5]

OECD (2023), *Biodiversity and Development Finance 2015-2021: Progress towards Target 19 of the Kunming-Montreal Global Biodiversity Framework*, OECD Publishing, https://doi.org/10.1787/6d43b54d-en. [4]

OECD (2021), *OECD DAC Declaration on a new approach to align development co-operation*, https://www.oecd.org/dac/development-assistance-committee/dac-declaration-climate-change-cop26.pdf (accessed on 1 July 2024). [8]

OECD (2020), *A Comprehensive Overview of Global Biodiversity Finance*, https://www.oecd.org/environment/resources/biodiversity/report-a-comprehensive-overview-of-global-biodiversity-finance.pdf (accessed on 1 July 2024). [7]

Notes

[1] The list of developed country Parties and other Parties that voluntarily assume the obligations of developed country parties to the CBD includes: Australia, Austria, Belgium, Canada, Czech Republic, Denmark, Finland, France, Germany, Greece, Iceland, Ireland, Italy, Japan, Luxembourg, Monaco, Netherlands, New Zealand, Norway, Portugal, Slovenia, Spain, Sweden, Switzerland and the United Kingdom (CBD, 2006[10]). It is important to note that this report also reflects contributions from additional bilateral providers, such as all OECD Development Assistance Committee (DAC) members (e.g. Estonia, EU institutions, Hungary, Korea, Lithuania, Poland, Slovak Republic, and the United States), and other non-DAC countries, see Annex A.

2 Total development finance for biodiversity

How does this report measure development finance for biodiversity?

Development finance for biodiversity can originate from several sources. Official development finance (ODF), which includes official development assistance (ODA) and other official flows (OOF), is one of these sources. Development finance can be either bilateral [e.g. directly provided by a Development Assistance Committee (DAC) member to recipient countries] or multilateral (resources channelled through and by international financial institutions, multilateral or regional development banks, and United Nations institutions). Development finance can also include other sources: bilateral providers beyond the DAC, including South-South and triangular co-operation providers; and private flows mobilised by public interventions. Private philanthropy is also a key source of development finance. This chapter provides estimates of the landscape of biodiversity-related development finance from all these sources. For further information on how these estimates were produced, see Box 2.1 and Annex A.

Box 2.1. Estimating biodiversity-related and biodiversity-specific development finance

This report uses a variety of data sources to estimate development finance for biodiversity, namely the OECD Development Assistance Committee's (DAC) *Creditor Reporting System* (CRS), which collects data on official development assistance and other official flows, as well as drawing from the *Total Official Support for Sustainable Development* (TOSSD) database. Countries and institutions reporting their official development finance signal flows to biodiversity-related activities using the biodiversity Rio marker, as well as through two Sustainable Development Goal (SDG) tags – SDG 14 and SDG 15.

For DAC members and countries and institutions reporting on the biodiversity marker, activities should be screened and marked as targeting the objectives of the Convention on Biological Diversity (CBD) as either a principal or significant objective; or not targeting the objective (the activity has no relation to the marker). Activities marked as "principal" must have biodiversity as fundamental in the design of, or the motivation for, the action. Activities marked "significant" have other primary objectives but have been formulated or adjusted to help meet biodiversity concerns.

The Rio Markers were designed to track the degree to which members are integrating and mainstreaming environmental considerations into their development co-operation activities, and thus apply to the entirety of an activity reported – not just the finance associated with the biodiversity-specific component of that activity. However, many DAC members apply a coefficient when reporting to the CBD on these flows, particularly to development finance that targets biodiversity as a "significant" objective [see (Casado-Asensio, Blaquier and Gualberti, 2024[1]) and Annex A for further information]. There is no agreed upon definition or common approach for this practice, but 40% is the most common coefficient applied to countries' "significant" flows.

The analysis in this report reflects two approaches: 1) "biodiversity-related development finance" which reflects the full value of flows reported to the OECD; and 2) "biodiversity-specific development finance", that applies a coefficient (40%) to flows corresponding to activities scoring as a "significant" (or secondary) objective of the biodiversity Rio marker and the totality (100%) of flows corresponding as "principal" (see Annex A for more information). The latter approach, therefore, provides a different scale but similar trends.

Total development finance for biodiversity has increased

Overall biodiversity-related development finance from all sources increased by 136% over 2015-22, rising from USD 10.9 billion in 2015 to USD 16.8 billion in 2021 and USD 25.8 billion in 2022 (or a USD 15.5 billion annual average over the period). Figure 2.1 shows biodiversity-related development finance flows over 2015-22 (USD 15.5 billion on average), reflecting the full value of all flows reported to the OECD (i.e. 100% of the flows tagged as both principal and significant). In particular, contributions from public sources (DAC members and other bilateral providers and multilateral providers) increased by 114%. This increase was largely driven by a significant increase by multilateral institutions, representing a 123% jump from 2021 to 2022. Overall, multilateral institutions made up to 33% of the total international public flows on average over 2015-22 while DAC members provided 67% of the total over this period (and mostly driven by ODA). Flows from other bilateral providers, including South-South and triangular co-operation providers, made up an additional 0.1% of the total and gained importance after 2017, when many of these providers started reporting to the OECD.

Overall biodiversity-specific development finance from all sources increased by 112% over 2015-22, rising from USD 7.3 billion in 2015 to USD 11.1 billion in 2021 and USD 15.4 billion in 2022 (USD 9.4 billion annual average over the period; Figure 2.2). International public development finance for biodiversity increased by 79% – also explained by the significant increase in contributions by multilateral institutions from 2021 to 2022. Overall, contributions from DAC members made up 72% of the total public flows on average over 2015-22, with the remaining 28% coming from multilateral institutions. Flows from other bilateral providers, including South-South and triangular co-operation, made up an additional 0.2% of the total.

Under both methodologies, private sources of development finance for biodiversity have been increasing over time (Figure 2.1 and Figure 2.2). Private philanthropic flows grew from USD 501 million in 2017 peaking at USD 932 million in 2021 and decreasing to USD 700 million in 2022. In turn, private finance flows mobilised by public interventions increased from USD 205 million in 2017, to USD 749 million in 2021 to reach USD 1.8 billion in 2022 and represented 72% of all private development finance for biodiversity in 2022. Figure 2.3 provides further details of the yearly breakdown of overall international public and private magnitudes, allowing to visualise and compare the two approaches, namely biodiversity-related (full values) and biodiversity-specific (estimates with coefficients).

Table 2.1 provides a breakdown of public biodiversity-related development finance from DAC members and multilateral institutions by type of flow and considering two approaches: biodiversity-related and biodiversity-specific. Biodiversity-related ODF reflects the full values of flows reported to the OECD while biodiversity-specific ODF applies coefficients to "significant" flows (see Annex A). The analysis shows that over 2015 to 2022, on average, DAC members' contributions were distributed mainly through ODA, with OOF growing progressively over the decade. Conversely, multilateral institutions' contributions were mostly provided through non-concessional flows.

Figure 2.1. Overall biodiversity-related development finance

2015-22, USD billion, full values

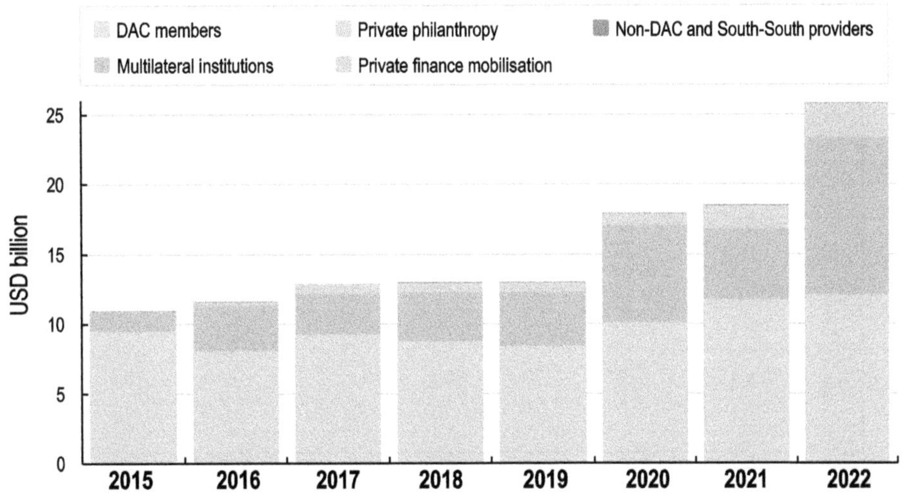

Notes: The figure shows the full value of all flows reported to the OECD. For details on what is covered under each category, see Annex A.
Source: Authors' estimates based on OECD-DAC statistics from OECD (2024[2]), *Creditor Reporting System* (database), https://data-explorer.oecd.org/s/c and on mobilised private finance from OECD (2024[3]), http://data-explorer.oecd.org/s/q, and *Total Official Support for Sustainable Development* (database) from TOSSD (2024[4]), https://www.tossd.org.

Figure 2.2. Overall biodiversity-specific development finance

2015-22, USD billion, estimates with coefficients

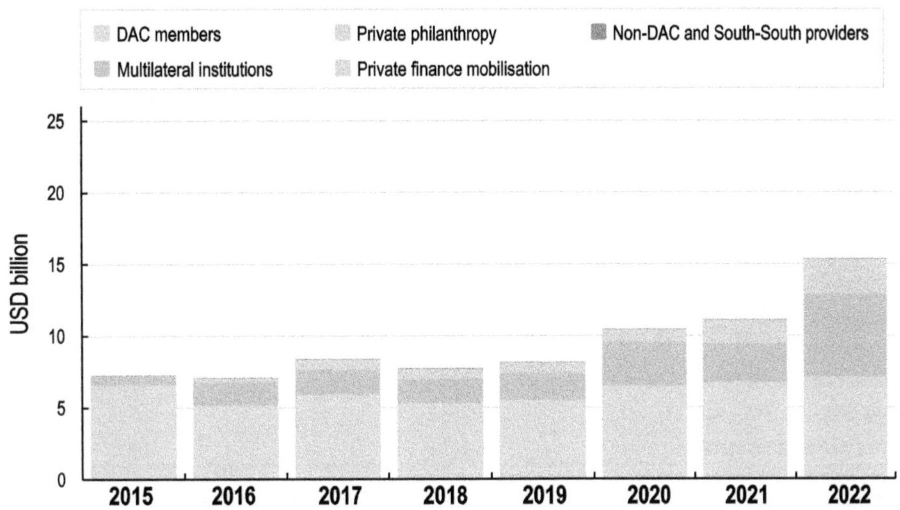

Notes: The figure shows coefficients applied to the information reported to the OECD. For DAC members, this implies taking the full value of flows marked as principal against the Rio marker flows and using a 40% coefficient for flows marked as significant against the Rio marker as well as flows identified as contributing to Sustainable Development Goals 14 and 15 (see Box 2.1). Multilateral institutions' activities reflect the full value of their core (principal and "principal-like") activities and apply a coefficient for activities considered as secondary (significant and "significant-like"). Information from private sources and non-DAC members and South-South providers reflect full values, hence they represent the same flows in Figure 2.1 and Figure 2.2. For methodological information and details on data coverage and sources, see Annex A.
Sources: Authors' estimates based on OECD-DAC statistics from OECD (2024[2]), *Creditor Reporting System* (database), https://data-explorer.oecd.org/s/c and on mobilised private finance from OECD (2024[3]), http://data-explorer.oecd.org/s/q, and *Total Official Support for Sustainable Development* (database) from TOSSD (2024[4]), https://www.tossd.org.

Figure 2.3. Development finance for biodiversity trends

2015-22, USD billion, biodiversity-related (full values) and biodiversity-specific (estimates with coefficients)

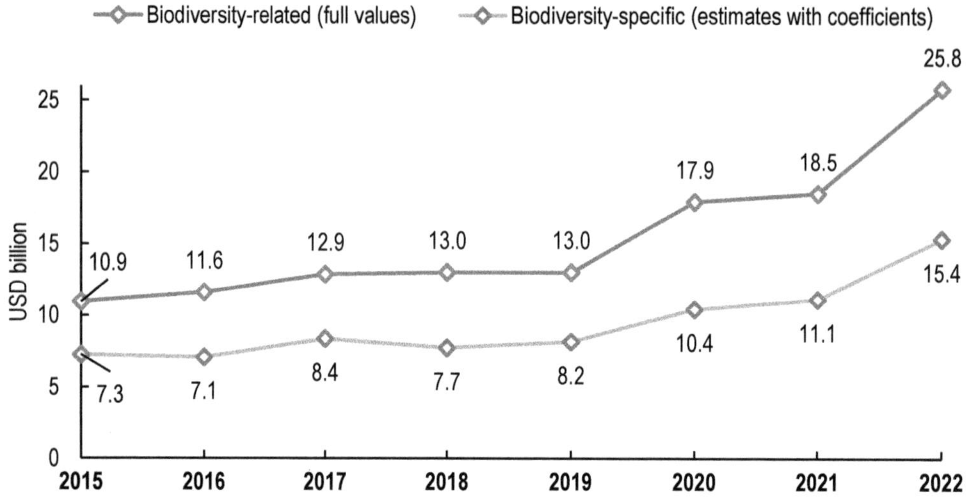

Notes: The biodiversity-related (blue) line shows the full value of all flows reported to the OECD. The biodiversity-specific (green) line shows coefficients applied to the information reported to the OECD. For annual data on the breakdown of each source of biodiversity-related development finance, see Annex C.

Sources: Authors' estimates based on OECD-DAC statistics from OECD (2024[2]), *Creditor Reporting System* (database), https://data-explorer.oecd.org/s/c and on mobilised private finance from OECD (2024[3]), http://data-explorer.oecd.org/s/q, and *Total Official Support for Sustainable Development* (database) from TOSSD (2024[4]), https://www.tossd.org.

Table 2.1. International public development finance for biodiversity

2015-22 annual average, bilateral and multilateral providers, USD million

Breakdown	Biodiversity-specific official development finance (estimates with coefficients)	Biodiversity-related official development finance (full values)
DAC members		
Official development assistance	5 910.7	9 370.8
Other official flows	193.6	376.6
DAC members total	6 104.3	9 747.4
Multilateral institutions		
Concessional finance	1 173.1	2 317.2
Non-concessional finance	1 213.6	2 449.7
Multilateral total	2 386.7	4 766.8
Total bilateral and multilateral	**8 491.0**	**14 514.2**

Notes: The table provides information on development finance reported to the OECD, including ranges corresponding to two approaches: biodiversity-related official development finance (ODF; i.e. which considers full values) and biodiversity-specific ODF (i.e. applying coefficients). For DAC members, biodiversity-specific ODF implies taking the full value of principal Rio marked flows and using a 40% coefficient for significant biodiversity Rio marked and additional Sustainable Development Goals (SDGs) 14 and 15 and biodiversity-related keywords. Multilateral activities reflect the full value of their core (principal and "principal-like") activities and apply a 40% coefficient for activities considered as secondary (significant and "significant-like"). Multilateral flows include principal, "principal-like", significant and "significant-like" data from a variety of sources, including Rio marker data on biodiversity, purpose code data, SDGs 14 and 15 data, and data captured through keyword search. For more information on the methodology used to obtain and analyse multilateral institutions' data, please consult Annex A.

Sources: Authors' estimates based on OECD-DAC statistics from OECD (2024[2]), *Creditor Reporting System* (database), https://data-explorer.oecd.org/s/c and *Total Official Support for Sustainable Development* (database) from TOSSD (2024[4]), https://www.tossd.org.

References

Casado-Asensio, J., D. Blaquier and G. Gualberti (2024), "Stock Take Report on Members' Reporting Practices on Biodiversity-related Development Finance and Reporting against International Obligations", *DCD/DAC/ENV(2024)1/REV1/FINAL*, https://one.oecd.org/document/DCD/DAC/ENV(2024)1/REV1/FINAL/en/pdf. [1]

OECD (2024), *OECD DAC Creditor Reporting System Statistics*, OECD.Stat, https://data-explorer.oecd.org/s/c. [2]

OECD (2024), "OECD Data Explorer", *Mobilised private finance for development*, http://data-explorer.oecd.org/s/q. [3]

TOSSD (2024), *Total Official Support for Sustainable Development*, https://www.tossd.org/. [4]

3 DAC members' development finance for biodiversity

Development Assistance Committee (DAC) members are the largest providers of bilateral development finance for biodiversity – using both the biodiversity-related and biodiversity-specific approaches (see Box 2.1). DAC members' biodiversity-related development finance increased from USD 9.5 billion in 2015 to USD 11.8 billion in 2021 and USD 12.1 billion in 2022 (Figure 3.1). This represents an annual average of USD 9.7 billion and 7% of total development finance flows, increasing by 3% in 2022 compared to 2021 values. When accounting for flows based on the use of coefficients, DAC members' biodiversity-specific development finance shows a similar trend, increasing from USD 6.6 billion in 2015 to USD 6.7 billion in 2021 and USD 7.1 in 2022 (Figure 3.2). This represents an annual average of USD 6.1 billion and 4% of total development finance flows. Estimates for 2022 increased by 6% compared to 2021 values.

This growing trend is also accompanied by members' commitments to deliver on a range of biodiversity-related development finance pledges (see Box 3.1); however, the percentage of biodiversity-related development finance has remained relatively stable in a context where DAC member official development finance (ODF) has grown. Further, despite the overall growth, the portion that is Rio-marked with biodiversity as a principal objective decreased between 2015 and 2022 by 17% (from USD 4.6 billion to USD 3.8 billion). While the trend was partly reversed from 2021 to 2022 when it increased by 21%, from USD 3.2 billion to USD 3.8 billion, it will be important that ODF for biodiversity with a principal objective continues to grow and remains constant to ensure the impacts of funded biodiversity-related activities are sustained over time.

The proportion of total biodiversity-related ODF targeting several objectives, i.e. activities marked with biodiversity as a significant objective, has been increasing over time in both methodologies by 69% from 2015 to 2022. This increase reflects greater attention to, or interest in, integrating biodiversity-related aspects across development co-operation activities and may reflect growing mainstreaming of biodiversity.

Figure 3.1. DAC members' biodiversity-related official development finance

2015-22, USD billion, full values

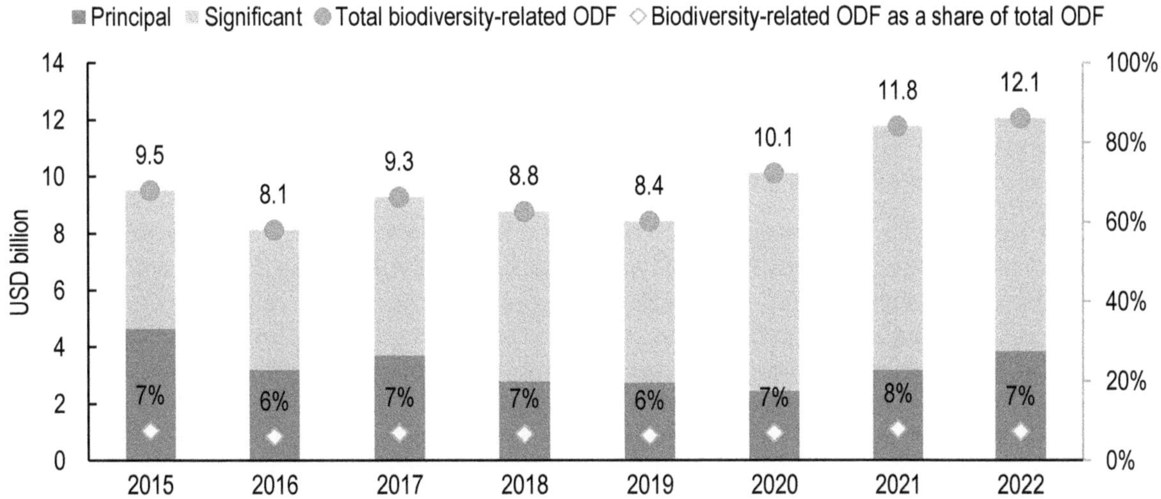

Notes: ODF: official development finance. For practical reasons, biodiversity-related development finance captured through the use of Sustainable Development Goals 14 and/or 15, as well as relevant keywords (reflected as "additional" in previous reports) are now reflected within the significant-like contributions. "Additional" allocations represent 6% of the total over the period reviewed.
Source: Authors' estimates based on OECD-DAC statistics from OECD (2024[1]), *Creditor Reporting System* (database), https://data-explorer.oecd.org/s/c.

Figure 3.2. DAC members' biodiversity-specific official development finance

2015-22, USD billion, estimates with coefficients

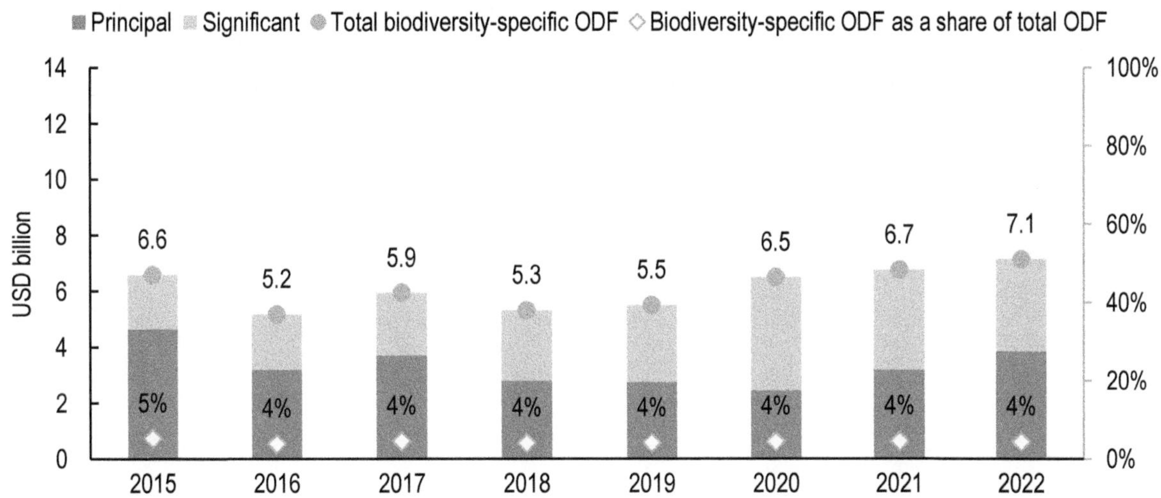

Notes: ODF: official development finance. The figure shows that Development Assistance Committee members' biodiversity-specific ODF is increasing even with coefficients. For practical reasons, biodiversity-related development finance captured through the use of Sustainable Development Goals 14 and/or 15, as well as relevant keywords (reflected as "additional" in previous reports) are now reflected within the significant-like contributions. "Additional" allocations represent 1% of the total over the period reviewed.
Source: Authors' estimates based on OECD-DAC statistics from OECD (2024[1]), *Creditor Reporting System* (database), https://data-explorer.oecd.org/s/c.

Box 3.1. Examples of progress on biodiversity-related development finance pledges

In 2021, at the United Nations Framework Convention on Climate Change COP26, 12 public donors endorsed the Global Forest Finance Pledge (GFFP), collectively committing to supporting countries to tackle the causes of deforestation (UK COP26, 2021[2]). Despite a turbulent global economy in the last few years, results suggest a steady trajectory towards achieving the 2025 target: in the first two years of the five-year pledge, USD 5.7 billion, or 47% of the USD 12 billion pledge, has already been directed towards forest-related programmes in developing countries (GFFP, 2023[3]). Overall, the GFFP contributions support activities that address the systemic drivers of forest loss, enabling the conservation, sustainable management and restoration of their forests, and in their climate mitigation and adaptation. Enabling the participation of Indigenous peoples and local communities (IPs and LCs) is also central to the activities contributing to the pledge.

Other forest pledges were also made at COP26 which are related to the GFFP[1] and over the same period, but distinct and supported by different types of donors as well, including both governments and private philanthropies. For instance, the Indigenous Peoples and Local Communities Forest Tenure Pledge is supported by 22 funders, committing to deliver USD 1.7 billion in support of advancing IPs and LCs forest tenure rights in tropical forest countries (COP26 Presidency, 2021[4]), with 48% provided by 2022 (FTFG, 2023[5]). This Pledge is further supported by the Forest Tenure Funders Group, an informal donor working group that facilitates donor co-ordination and collaboration. Further, the Congo Basin Pledge is supported by 12 funders committing to provide USD 1.5 billion to protect, maintain and sustainably manage the Congo Basin forests and peatlands (UK COP26, 2021[6]), and with 70% provided by 2022 (CBFP, 2022[7]).

1. Given that public donor funding may contribute to the objectives of several commitments, the pledges cannot be aggregated or compared.

Biodiversity-related official development finance is primarily driven by five DAC members

Building upon the previous section, Figure 3.3 ranks the top DAC members according to their biodiversity-related and biodiversity-specific ODF. The main DAC members over 2015-22 were Germany, France, EU institutions, the United States and Japan, independent of the approach used, which together accounted for at least 73% of total biodiversity-related ODF. Most DAC member ODF is driven by ODA investments, which represents about 96% of total biodiversity-related ODF, and other offical flows (4%). In relative terms, biodiversity is most important in the programmes of France, Belgium, Sweden, Norway and Iceland, where estimates show that it represents upto 17%, 16%, 13%, 12% and 12% of their ODF activities, respectivey, followed by Italy, Australia and Germany, with 10-11% (see Figure 3.3).

Figure 3.3. Top donors of development finance for biodiversity

2015-22, commitments, USD billion, biodiversity-related (blue) and biodiversity-specific (pink)

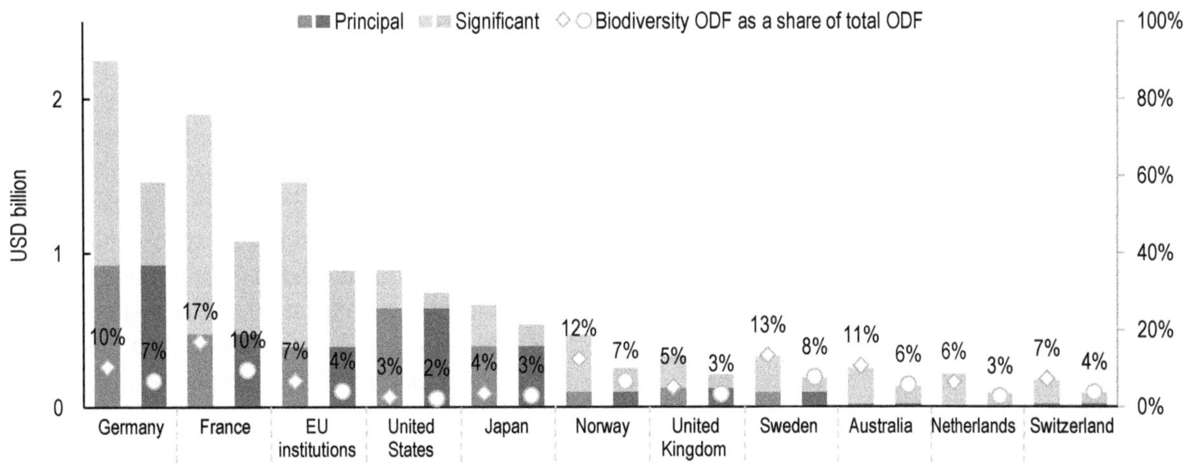

Notes: ODF: official development finance. Biodiversity-related (full values) development finance is represented with blue, while biodiversity-specific (estimates with coefficients) with pink.
Source: Authors' estimates based on OECD-DAC statistics from OECD (2024[1]), *Creditor Reporting System* (database), https://data-explorer.oecd.org/s/c.

DAC members' development co-operation efforts cover a wide range of priorities. They provide development finance to developing countries – through intermediaries and/or direct access – engaging with various partners at multiple levels, including municipal authorities, trade unions, universities, non-governmental organisations, Indigenous peoples' organisations, and civil society [e.g. through decentralised co-operation (OECD, 2019[8])]. Many investments aimed at achieving the SDGs would benefit from locally led action, yet require support for their implementation and a significant increase of domestic resource mobilisation. Box 3.2 shows how DAC members are contributing to address this challenge, by enhancing enabling environments and supporting the development of local capacities, for example, to develop National Biodiversity Strategies and Actions Plans (NBSAPs) or national biodiversity finance plans [i.e. Target 19(b) of the Kunming-Montreal Global Biodiversity Framework (KMGBF)].

Box 3.2. DAC members' efforts to support enabling environments and domestic resource mobilisation

Conducive enabling environments and increased investment are key to halting and reversing biodiversity loss. Development Assistance Committee (DAC) members make significant efforts to strengthen enabling environments, including by co-operating on developing local capacities, encouraging sector- and region-specific policies and strategies, and alleviating the wider constraints to private investment (OECD, 2023[9]). Ultimately, these steps are key for both international and domestic resource mobilisation.

For example, the United States is assisting the United Republic of Tanzania to address major threats related to wildlife by building the institutional capacities of both public and private stakeholders; improving the policy, regulatory and enabling environment for biodiversity conservation and natural resource management; and increasing private sector engagement in this space (USAID, 2024[10]).

USAID is also supporting Peru to enhance forest sector governance by building national capacity in forest management and strengthening the enabling environment, contributing to low emissions development and addressing deforestation (USAID, 2022[11]). This includes providing technical assistance in tropical forest management and regulations, supporting regulatory authorities in organisational development, developing strategic public financing mechanisms to strengthen the legal framework on forest resources, and improving evidence-based decision making on natural resource management.

At the United Nations Biodiversity Conference (CBD COP15), under the leadership of Colombia and Germany, an NBSAP Accelerator Partnership (NBSAP Accelerator Partnership, 2024[12]) was announced with the aim of accelerating the implementation of NBSAPs by providing or facilitating access to financial and technical support, and through match-making and resource mobilisation support, identifying country-specific biodiversity priorities and capacity needs, and peer-to-peer learning. Germany and Norway contribute to the creation and operationalisation of the platform with funding, as well as by providing knowledge management and help desk support services to members of the NBSAP Accelerator Partnership (GIZ, 2024[13]; NBSAP Accelerator Partnership, 2024[12]).

Similarly, through the United Nations Development Programme's Biodiversity Finance Initiative (BIOFIN, 2021[14]), supported by Belgium, Canada, the European Union, France, Germany, Norway, Switzerland, and the United Kingdom, members support the development of transformative policy and financing frameworks to increase investment in biodiversity management across developing countries. It aims to support capacity development and effective mobilisation of financial resources for the protection and sustainable use of biodiversity, including through supporting a global campaign to repurpose harmful subsidies, accelerating the implementation of national biodiveristy finance plans and developing a biodiveristy expenditure taxonomy to support biodiversity finance planning.

Middle-income countries receive the most biodiversity-related bilateral official development finance

About a fourth of total biodiversity-related ODF is concentrated in the top five recipients of bilateral biodiversity-related ODF: Colombia, India, Ukraine, Ethiopia and Indonesia (see Figure 3.4). In particular, the top recipients of contributions targeting activities with biodiversity as a core objective are Colombia, India, Ukraine, Mexico and the Democratic Republic of the Congo, on average over 2015-22. Although most biodiversity-related development finance tends to be concentrated around the same top recipients over this period, allocations towards partner countries also vary yearly and, most recently, Mexico, Peru, Morocco and Costa Rica also stand out over 2021-22. In relative terms, biodiversity-related interventions are particularly relevant in other countries, notably Saint Lucia, Republic of the Congo and Guyana, where they represented 57%, 44% and 41% of their total ODF investments, respectively, on average over 2015-22. However, in most recipients, biodiversity-related considerations are integrated into less than 10% of ODF received.

Overall, among the top ten recipients are countries that include biodiversity hotspots, which are recognised as the Earth's most biologically diverse yet threatened areas (CEPF, 2024[15]). For example, Colombia encompasses the Tumbes-Chocó-Magdalena and Tropical Andes biodiversity hotspots while India is home to the Western Ghats and Himalaya, and Ethiopia the Horn of Africa and Eastern Afromontane biodiversity hotspots. These countries not only host irreplaceable biodiversity but also face significant challenges such as habitat loss, climate change and unsustainable resource extraction. As such, biodiversity-related development finance can help partner countries protect ecosystems; preserve natural heritage; enhance environmental resilience; and empower local communities to sustainably manage natural resources, foster social cohesion, bolster local economies and support income while promoting capacity development, livelihood opportunities and community well-being.

Figure 3.4. Top recipients of DAC members' biodiversity-related development finance

2015-22, USD million, full values

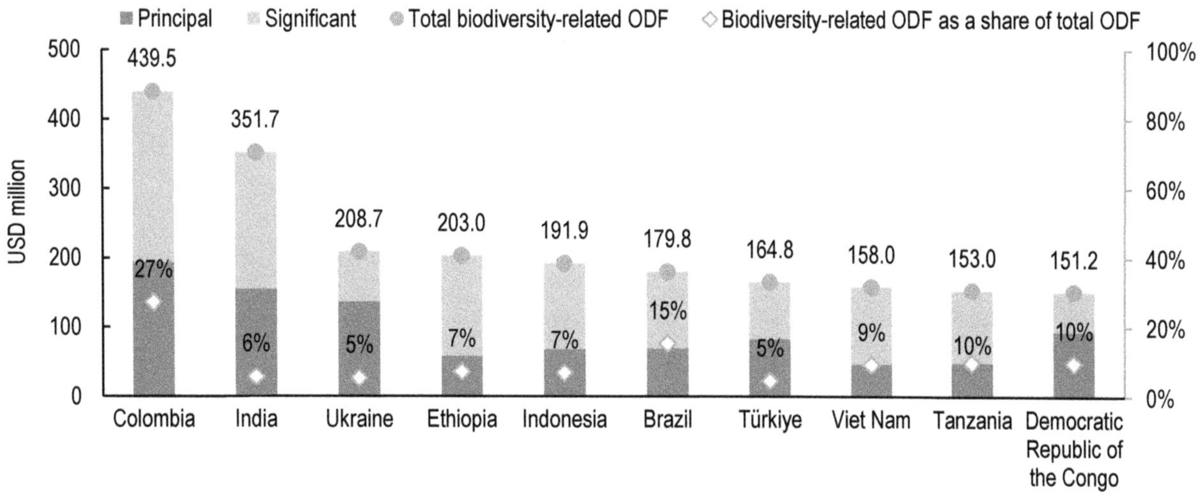

Notes: ODF: official development finance. ODF for biodiversity from DAC members is concentrated around the same top 10 recipients both for the biodiversity-related and biodiversity-specific approaches on average over 2015-22. This analysis excludes unspecified and regional allocations which accounted for USD 3.7 billion, or 37%, of total bilateral biodiversity-related flows.

Source: Authors' estimates based on OECD-DAC statistics from OECD (2024[1]), *Creditor Reporting System* (database), https://data-explorer.oecd.org/s/c.

Most biodiversity-related ODF targets middle-income countries (MICs). In fact, on average over 2015-22, lower middle-income countries (LMICs) received 37% of bilateral funds for biodiversity while upper middle-income countries (UMICs) received 30%. Meanwhile, least developed countries (LDCs) and other low-income countries (LICs) received 33% of bilateral funds. In relative terms, the share of biodiversity-related contributions towards LDCs and other LICs is slightly lower than when looking at total ODF over the period (37%). While indeed biodiversity hotspots are often concentrated in MICs, the development and stability of LDCs and other LICs can also be significantly dependent upon biodiversity and natural resources (OECD, 2023[16]; IPBES, 2019[17]), and would benefit from biodiversity-related development finance. Nonetheless, development finance for biodiversity out of total ODF remains low, irrespective of income level (5% for LDCs and other LICs and 7% for MICs).

Biodiversity-related development finance received by small island developing states (SIDS) was USD 324 million on average annually over 2015-22, representing 10% of total ODF received by this group (which is above the total allocable country share of 6%). Moreover, SIDS received 5% of total biodiversity-related ODF from DAC members, and slightly above overall ODF trends to SIDS (at 3% over 2015-22). According to the OECD's classification, SIDS that are LDCs received 33% of the total while LMICs received 29% and 37% went to UMICs. Several SIDS countries received significant shares of biodiversity-related flows out of total ODF from DAC members: Saint Lucia (57% of all ODF received), Guyana (41%), Suriname (27%), Cuba (24%), Tuvalu (20%), Guinea-Bissau (19%), Papua New Guinea (13%), Palau (11%) and Mauritius (11%).

Africa and Asia are the regions benefiting most from biodiversity-related official development finance

In terms of regions, Africa (at USD 2.9 billion, 30% of the total) and Asia (USD 2 billion, 21% of the total) are the regions that received the most biodiversity-related ODF over 2015-22 (Figure 3.5). This trend was followed by Latin America and the Caribbean (LAC, USD 1.7 billion, or 17% of the total). In effect, Africa was the region targeted the most every year during this period, followed by Asia (with the exception of 2017 and 2021 when LAC came out in second place). While the share towards Africa remained stable compared to the portion of total ODF (32%), the biodiversity-related shares are relatively lower for Asia (32%) and higher than the overall share to LAC (8%). Oceania saw the largest growth rate of biodiversity-related development finance allocated over the period (75%), followed by LAC (44%). In contrast, flows to Europe decreased by 70% in 2022 compared to 2015.

Figure 3.5. DAC members' biodiversity-related official development finance by region

2015-22, USD, full values

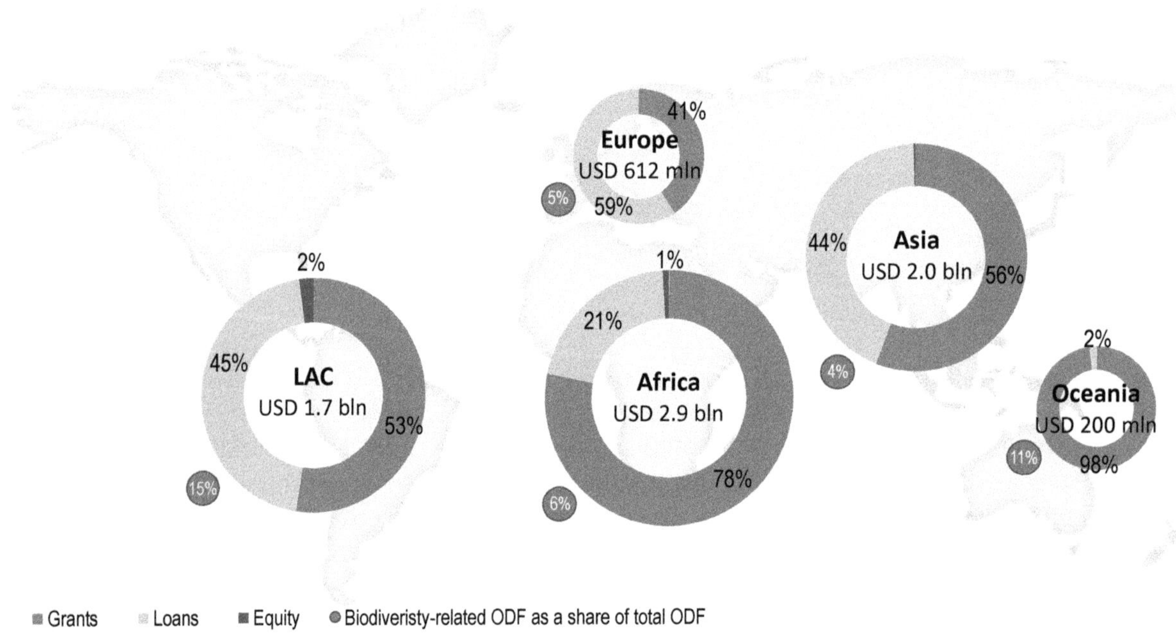

Notes: ODF: official development finance; LAC: Latin America and the Caribbean. Africa and Asia receive most DAC member biodiversity-related ODF. Financial instruments represented include: grants (e.g. standard grants); debt instruments (e.g. standard loans, reimbursable grants and other debt securities); and equity (e.g. common equity and shares in collective investment vehicles). About 24%, or USD 2.3 billion, of biodiversity-related ODF falls into the "unallocated" by region category, i.e. it is not earmarked to a country or region, and so has not been included in this analysis.
Source: Authors' estimates based on OECD-DAC statistics from OECD (2024[1]), *Creditor Reporting System* (database), https://data-explorer.oecd.org/s/c.

In terms of financial instruments, the predominant channels used by bilateral providers are grants (68%), followed by loans (31%) and, to a lesser extent equity (1%), over 2015-22. However, the composition of financial instruments used varied across DAC members. Grants represented most commitments at an individual level, constituting more than 90% of at least two-thirds of DAC members' total biodiversity-related development finance, except for a few cases where loans were the main instrument: France (87%), Poland (85%), Japan (81%) and Canada (51%). Equity was mainly used in the cases of Finland (28%), Austria

(10%) and Italy (7%), while other members also made use of other types of finance: the United Kingdom through subordinated loans, Canada preferred equity and France guarantees.

Overall, most grants are directed to LDCs and other LICs (47%), followed by LMICs (31%) and UMICs (22%), whereas loans are mostly concentrated in LMICs and UMICs (45% and 42%) and to a lesser degree towards LDCs and other LICs (13%). In relative terms, the shares of financial instruments varied across income groups and regions. For instance, grants are predominantly used in LDCs and LICs (83% of bilateral flows), and especially in Oceania (98% of bilateral flows are in the form of grants) and Africa (78%). Europe is the region that receives most contributions in the form of loans (59%). In turn, while allocations to MICs tend to involve loans and grants more evenly, most of their funding is channelled through loans (50% and 58%, for LMICs and UMICs respectively).

Biodiversity could be mainstreamed further into all official development finance nature-dependent sectors

In volume terms, the main sectors targeted by bilateral biodiversity-related ODF are general environmental protection (31%), agriculture (15%) and water (12%, including water supply and sanitation) (Figure 3.6). In particular, 40% of biodiversity-related ODF targeting the general environmental protection dimension corresponds to the biodiversity policy domain itself. In most cases, biodiversity-related activities have been mainstreamed (captured by the significant marker), except in the general environment protection and forestry sectors, where they mostly represent the core objective of the activities.

Figure 3.6. DAC members' biodiversity-related official development finance by sector

2015-22, USD billion, full values

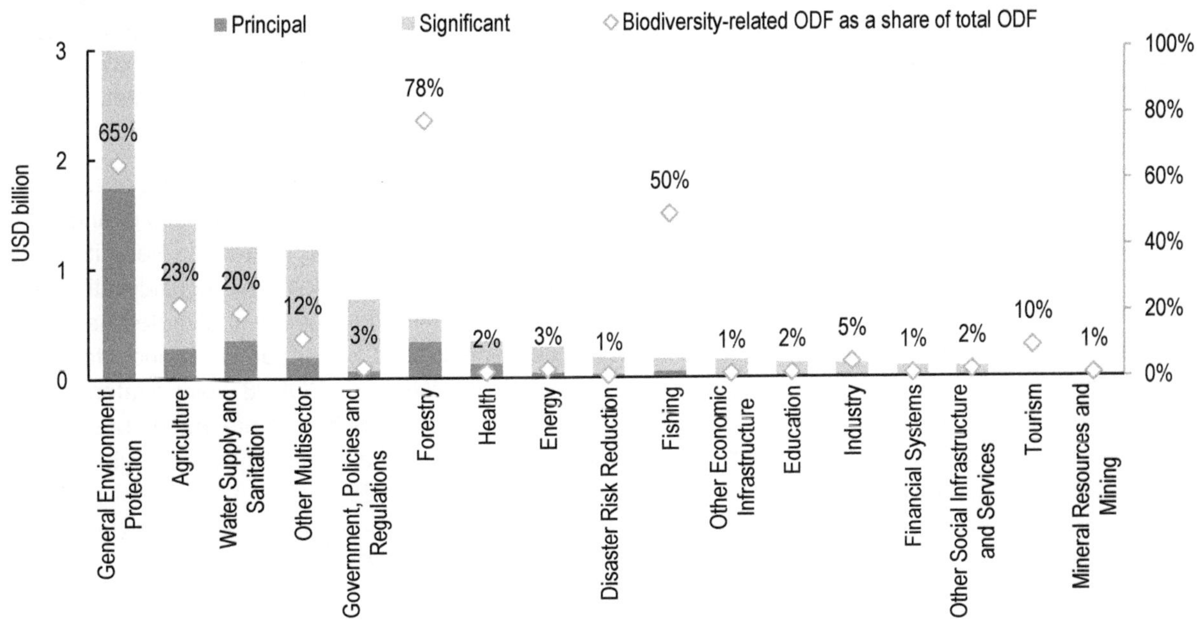

Notes: ODF: official development finance. About 1%, or USD 109 million, of biodiversity-related ODF falls into the "unallocated" category, i.e. it is not earmarked to a sector, and so has not been included in this analysis. For further information on the classification of socio-economic areas, please consult Annex A.
Source: Authors' estimates based on OECD-DAC statistics from OECD (2024[1]), *Creditor Reporting System* (database), https://data-explorer.oecd.org/s/c.

At an aggregate level, biodiversity-related ODF represents 7% of total ODF. However, this share varies across sectors ranging from 78% in activities related to forestry to 65% in general environment protection, 50% in fishing and less than 23% in all other sectors – including nature-dependent sectors [e.g. agriculture (23%), water supply and sanitation (20%), mineral resources and mining (1%)]. Indeed, many sectors that are key for development in developing countries are dependent on nature, such as agriculture, forestry, fishing, construction, mining, electricity, chemicals, materials and tourism, e.g. relying on either direct extraction of resources from forests or oceans or the provision of ecosystem services such as healthy soils, clean water, pollination and a stable climate (WEF, 2020[18]). As nature loses its capacity to provide such services, these sectors could suffer significant losses, and so would the livelihoods of those that depend on them to survive. This trend reveals the potential scope for increasing biodiversity-related ODF across their interventions, an issue that the OECD and DAC members are exploring in a forthcoming report that looks at the alignment of development co-operation with the KMGBF (OECD, forthcoming).

Climate investments dominate biodiversity-related official development finance, representing opportunities to seek co-benefits and reduce trade-offs

The share of DAC members' biodiversity-related bilateral ODF that also targets climate change on average over 2015-22 was 83% (or USD 8.1 billion) (Figure 3.7). More than half of this supports activities that jointly target climate change adaptation and mitigation objectives (USD 4.2 billion). This points to how DAC members seek synergies through their biodiversity- and climate-related development finance. However, only 20% of climate-related development finance targeted biodiversity specifically on average over the period - and this share decreased from 24% in 2015 to 19% in 2022 (accounting for USD 7.5 billion and USD 11.1 billion, respectively) (Figure 3.8). This could be partly due to the increasing attention to climate change, including more ambitious climate change resource mobilisation targets [e.g. the United Nations Framework Convention on Climate Change's (UNFCCC) climate finance goal of USD 100 billion was exceeded in 2022 (OECD, 2024[19]), while the KMGBF aims for USD 25 billion by 2030 (CBD, 2022[20])], and to the opportunities to address climate change objectives through activities benefiting ecosystems, while many necessary climate actions do not necessarily target biodiversity (e.g. renewables, energy efficiency).

Given the relatively larger volumes targeting climate-related objectives (USD 39.8 billion on average over 2015-22, by DAC members only) and the intricate links between biodiversity loss and climate change, it is important to seek opportunities to better integrate biodiversity considerations and co-benefits while ensuring that climate activities do not undermine biodiversity-related objectives. This consideration is in line with Targets 8 and 19(e) of the KMGBF, which seek to minimise the impact of climate change on biodiversity while building resilience, and to optimise co-benefits and synergies of finance targeting biodiversity and climate, respectively (CBD, 2022[20]); with the UNFCCC COP28 Joint Statement on Climate, Nature and People, committing to scaling finance and investments for climate and nature from all sources in a synergetic manner that ensures the promotion of co-benefits and efficient use through nature-based solutions and/or ecosystem based approaches (UNFCCC COP28, 2023[21]); and with the UAE Framework for Global Climate Resilience, seeking to reduce climate impacts on ecosystems and biodiversity and to accelerate the use of nature-based solutions (UNFCCC, 2023[22]).

Figure 3.7. Biodiversity and climate-related official development finance out of total biodiversity-related official development finance

2015-22, USD billion, full values

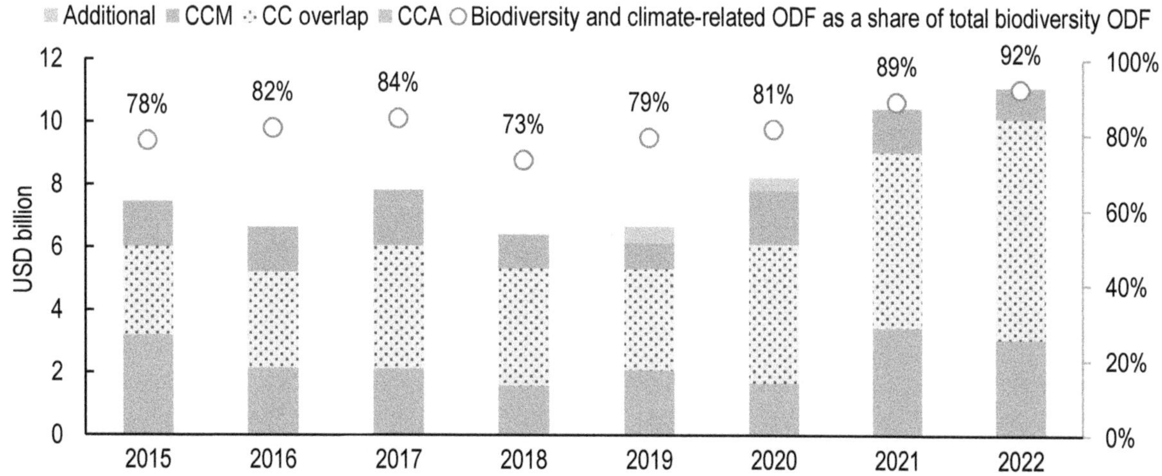

Notes: ODF: official development finance; CCA: climate change adaptation; CCM: climate change mitigation; CC overlap: activities targeting both climate change adaptation and mitigation objectives simultaneously. Additional refers to activities captured through Sustainable Development Goal 13 that could not be disaggregated by type of climate objective.
Source: Authors' estimates based on OECD-DAC statistics from OECD (2024[1]), *Creditor Reporting System* (database), https://data-explorer.oecd.org/s/c.

Figure 3.8. Climate and biodiversity-related official development finance out of total climate-related official development finance

2015-22, USD billion, full values

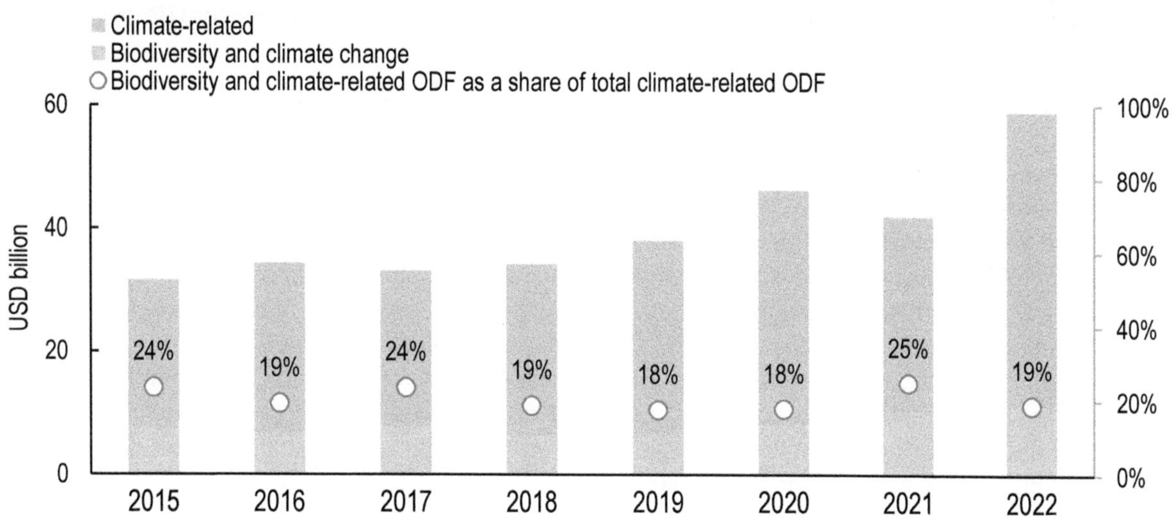

Note: ODF: official development finance.
Source: Authors' estimates based on OECD-DAC statistics from OECD (2024[1]), *Creditor Reporting System* (database), https://data-explorer.oecd.org/s/c.

Analysis by PricewaterhouseCoopers has found that about half of the world's total gross domestic product is highly or moderately dependent on nature and its ecosystem services (PwC, 2023[23]). As a result, it is exposed to risks from nature loss, which can severely affect the economy (WEF, 2020[24]). The World Economic Forum has classified extreme weather events, critical changes to Earth systems, biodiversity loss and ecosystem collapse, and natural resource shortages as the top four most severe global risks over the next decade (WEF, 2024[25]). Rapid and scaled-up action is therefore vital to halt and reverse the decline of natural capital and to fight climate change – two challenges that are intertwined and must be addressed together (Box 3.3). Ultimately, the effectiveness of development finance, as well as maximising co-benefits between financing for biodiversity, poverty reduction and broader developent outcomes, could play an important role in accelerating progress towards the achievement of the SDGs and ensuring that every invesment counts in an increasingly resource-constrained world.

Box 3.3. Breaking the silos: Integrating synergies across Rio Conventions and the Sustainable Development Goals

Biodiversity loss, climate change and land degradation pose existential threats to nature and humanity, and are strongly interlinked. Actions to address them must be interlinked and co-ordinated, seeking to achieve the Sustainable Development Goals (SDGs) by tackling them together. The efficiency gains of joint prioritisation underscore the mutual benefits that arise from bridging the aims of the three Rio Conventions rather than pursuing their objectives in isolation (UNCCD, 2022[26]). However, efforts to address these challenges, both internationally and nationally, have evolved in silos.

Development finance seeking co-benefits between biodiversity and climate-related objectives has increased in volume (Figure 3.9), climate-related only finance has increased as well, yet biodiversity-related finance only decreased in 2022 compared to 2015. In effect, the climate-related official development finance part that does not consider biodiversity issues has doubled, while the biodiversity only part has halved. Indeed, there is a growing concern that activities targeting climate change objectives may be detrimental for biodiversity, further frustrating existing biodiversity commitments. This reflects what some analysts call the "climatisation" of nature that risks overshadowing attention to other values (e.g. genetic diversity, wildlife protection, other non-carbon ecosystem services) (Parrotta et al., 2022[27]).

As nature-based solutions (NbS) are hailed as a pathway for promoting synergies between the climate change and biodiversity agendas (Pettorelli et al., 2021[28]), caution will be needed to ensure that biodiversity benefits, that are essential for any action to qualify as NbS according to the United Nations Environment Assembly's (UNEA) definition are also delivered. In fact, there is a risk with over-simplistic design and implementation of NbS, which may not meet the United Nations Environment Assembly's definition (UNEP, 2022[29]). While actions claiming to be NbS can aim to address climate change, they may ultimately be harmful for biodiversity, and well-designed NbS need to not only respect social and environmental safeguards in line with the Rio Conventions but also further NbS standards in line with UNEA's definition, supporting nature and people together (Seddon et al., 2021[30]). Within this context, development co-operation has a dual role to play: 1) by seeking synergies (and avoiding trade-offs across its development co-operation strategies and finance; and 2) supporting partner countries in implementing projects in a synergistic manner.

Furthermore, while climate change is a key driver of biodiversity loss, some of the solutions to climate change can exacerbate risks for biodiversity. For example, recent OECD analyses show that, unless carefully planned and managed, climate-related finance and investment in the renewable energy sector could compromise biodiversity (OECD, 2024[31]). It is, therefore, important to not only seek synergies but also to carefully manage potential trade-offs by integrating biodiversity considerations early into planning processes and adhering to good practice principles.

Figure 3.9. The overlap between biodiversity and climate-related official development finance

2015 and 2022, USD billion, full values

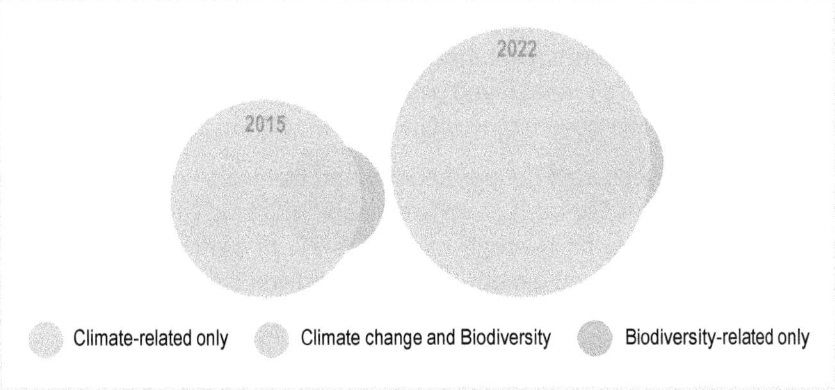

Note: The circles reflect official development finance (ODF) integrating climate-related only, biodiversity-related only, and both climate and biodiversity-related considerations for 2015 and 2022.
Source: Authors' estimates based on OECD-DAC statistics from OECD (2024[1]), *Creditor Reporting System* (database), https://data-explorer.oecd.org/s/c.

In April 2024, the UNEA-6 resolution highlighted the need to enhance the synergistic implementation of different multilateral environmental agreements and other relevant environmental instruments – including the Paris Agreement and the Kunming-Montreal Global Biodiversity Framework (KMGBF) (UNEP, 2024[32]). Further, the Rio Convention secretariats of the United Nations Framework Convention on Climate Change, Convention on Biological Diversity and Convention to Combat Desertification launched a Joint Capacity-building Programme to help policy makers and practitioners to better seize synergies among the Rio Conventions and the SDGs, focusing on partner engagement and the sharing of best practices.

Given the political momentum with the three Rio Conventions' COPs coming up, and the Summit of the Future set to deliberate on a path forward to transition to more co-operative approaches to global governance in 2024, action could consider opportunities to strengthen synergies and minimise trade-offs between biodiversity, climate and land goals and targets. Importantly, realising the ambitions of the SDGs requires a whole-of-government and whole-of-society approach [as particularly noted in the KMGBF (CBD, 2024[33])], with contributions from all actors – public, private and civil society organisations – at global and national levels.

Gender equality is key for development, biodiversity and the sustainable use of natural resources

Women often play a vital role in managing natural resources: promoting sustainable agriculture, forestry and fisheries; and advocating for environmental protection (CBD, n.d.[34]), and considering gender dimensions in biodiversity-related decision making can lead to positive outcomes for biodiversity and gender equality. Targets 22 and 23 of the KMGBF recognise the need to ensure gender equality in the implementation of the framework through a gender-responsive approach, whereby women and girls have the opportunity to contribute to the three objectives of the CBD, including by recognising their equal rights and access to land and natural resources, and their representation and informed participation in decision making related to biodiversity (CBD, n.d.[35]; CBD, n.d.[34]). Further, the CBD Gender Plan of Action (GPA) provides a roadmap for ensuring a rights-based gender-responsive implementation of the KMGBF, recognising the importance of advancing efforts to achieve gender equality and women's and girl's empowerment (CBD, 2022[36]). The GPA also invites relevant stakeholders to provide technical and financial support (e.g. Objective 3.6), as well as capacity development, for its implementation by, for example: supporting women's organisations and networks to participate on policies related to land and waters, land tenure and property reforms; or supporting measures to facilitate equal access of women to financial services and credit, and of all women and girls to education, training, information and technologies relevant for their engagement in the governance, conservation and sustainable use of biodiversity.

In particular, funding that addresses both gender equality and biodiversity has been increasing over time, in both absolute and relative terms. Figure 3.10 shows that 58% of biodiversity-related DAC bilateral ODF also targets gender equality issues on average over 2015-22. In particular, the share of development finance addressing both biodiversity and gender equality objectives increased over this period, from 46% in 2015 to 66% in 2021 and 68% in 2022. However, the opposite does not hold true and only about 12% of development finance with gender equality objectives also aimed to integrate biodiversity-related concerns, both in 2021 and 2022. DAC members could continue to look for ways to integrate biodiversity and gender equality across development finance portfolios, considering the vital role that women play in the conservation and sustainable use of biological diversity, and the importance of their participation in related policy making and implementation [in line with specific actions from the GPA to ensure progress towards the achievement of Target 23 of the KMGBF (CBD, n.d.[34])].

In relative terms, Canada, the Netherlands and Iceland have mainstreamed gender equality objectives into more than 93% of their biodiversity-related development finance portfolio, followed by Ireland, Luxembourg, Sweden and Spain, which reflect over 75% integration on average over 2015-22. Projects that include both considerations can span across, for example, those supporting women's rights defenders from Indigenous and rural communities in their climate action, or those supporting efforts to improve women's rights for control and ownership of sustainable agricultural production and income.

Figure 3.10. Biodiversity-related and gender mainstreaming in development finance

2015-22, USD billion, full values

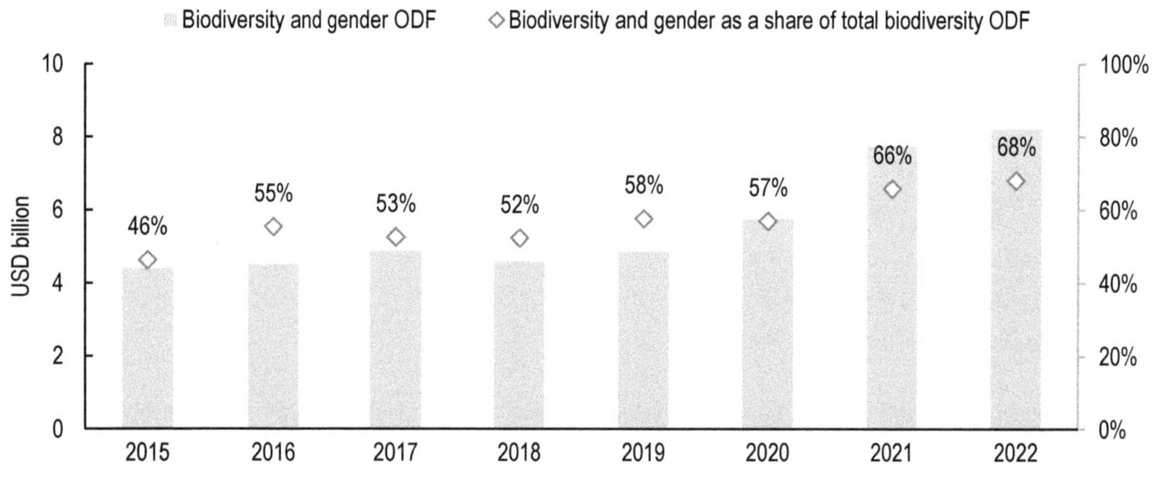

Notes: ODF: official development finance. Gender-related activities are captured both through the gender equality marker and Sustainable Development Goal 5 (see Annex A).

Source: Authors' estimates based on OECD-DAC statistics from OECD (2024[1]), *Creditor Reporting System* (database), https://data-explorer.oecd.org/s/c.

For instance, Spain is carrying out actions that advocate for women's leadership in rural and fishing areas, strengthening the capacities of Indigenous women to defend the land, and prioritising organisations and women defenders of common natural resources (AECID, 2022[37]). In particular, as part of a strategy to promote sustainable rural development by applying a gender approach, Spain has been supporting Mozambique in improving living conditions and environmental sustainability through the improvement of productive capacities based on sustainable mangrove management and the empowerment of women and youth affected by mangrove degradation (fishing and agriculture) (Cooperanda, 2021[38]). Additionally, they also support projects with a strong component of access to and control of resources, including with the purchase of land for women's collective use and access to credit, and the inclusion of gender equity in the implementation of land tenure legislation in rural communities (Cooperanda, 2019[39]).

Indigenous peoples and local communities are key partners to reduce biodiversity loss and environmental degradation

Sustainable development, biodiversity and climate action, and Indigenous peoples and local communities (IPs and LCs)[1] are often interdependent. Given their historical linkages to territories, their diverse worldviews and close relationship with, and as part of, nature, land and sea, these communities are important to the conservation, sustainable management and governance of biodiversity (e.g. conservation of watersheds, forest protection, sustainable land use), while nature directly underpins the livelihoods of Indigenous peoples and local communities, largely through direct consumption, income generated by trade of material resources (e.g. food, fibres, medicine, energy) or cultural links (e.g. spiritual, traditional knowledge, language). However, environmental degradation, exacerbated by climate change and pressures from activities such as "resource extraction, commodity production, mining and transport and energy infrastructure" (IPBES, 2019[17]), pose significant challenges. These factors, coupled with issues of lack of inclusion, limited participation, and restricted access to land and resources, not only erode the environment but also hinder sustainable development, resulting in further biodiversity loss and potential conflicts.

Addressing these interconnected challenges requires collective action. Biodiversity-related development finance can play an important role in supporting local efforts to mitigate environmental threats and promote the sustainable use of natural resources, contributing to safeguarding the environment and providing sustainable development opportunities for IPs and LCs. Understanding where the funds are going, and how much is reaching IPs and LCs, can help address local needs more effectively and support actions for biodiversity conservation and the sustainable management of natural resources (see Box 3.4).

Box 3.4. Challenges and opportunities of tracking development finance to the local ground

Transparent and reliable data are important to enable informed decision making; prioritise and allocate resources; and facilitate collaborations among Indigenous peoples and local communities (IPs and LCs), their allies and donors. Accurately tracking and reporting at the local level can also help understand how much funding effectively reaches the intended partners. Yet, data disclosure should also be accompanied by precautionary measures to protect IPs and LCs from potential risks, such as exposure to external pressures and influence, misinformation, discrimination and undermining their rights and sovereignty.

Tracking the financial contributions, including development finance, to IPs and LCs is particularly challenging, further exacerbated by the range of players that can be involved (e.g. providers, fiscal sponsors, national governments, civil society organisations). Moreover, while some funds channelled through the public sector and multilateral organisations may target IPs and LCs, transaction costs at each step can reduce the amount of funding that reaches or is managed by them (RFN, 2021[40]). The complexity of these processes, combined with the limited capacities of providers to interact directly with several IPs and LCs, further complicates effective tracking and reporting.

Addressing these challenges can support efforts to step up action and ambition on biodiversity. Increasing direct funding to IPs and LCs, along with strengthening their capacity to access and manage these resources, can help address local needs and support Indigenous-led solutions. This also includes navigating through bureaucracy, ensuring they meet due diligence, monitoring and transparency criteria, which are fundamental to the accountability of development finance. As such, direct access to funding, avoiding intermediaries, and drawing on traditional knowledge and leadership, are also key.

The importance of these issues has been further stressed through the recommendations of the United Nations Permanent Forum on Indigenous Issues (UNPFII) calling to increase direct funding, eliminate intermediaries where possible, and enhance accountability in financing for Indigenous peoples. In particular, the UNPFII recommends the OECD DAC to facilitate the tracking of funding in its statistical system[1]. The UNPFII has also invited DAC members to present progress in this area at the 24th session in 2025 [(UNPFII, 2024[41]; UNPFII, 2023[42])].

1. The recommendation alludes to tracking of finance including, and beyond, the context of development and biodiversity.

Identifying biodiversity-related ODF targeting IPs and LCs is not easy using the DAC CRS. Hence, for this report, a keyword search was used to identify bilateral DAC members' activities related to IPs and LCs in the context of development and biodiversity (see Annex B). The keyword search found that IP and LC-related projects received little ODF for biodiversity in 2022, namely USD 674 million, representing 6% of DAC members' total biodiversity-related ODF, mainly focusing on projects related to environmental protection, agriculture, policies and regulations, fishing, forestry, and tourism. This share is slightly higher than past assessments showing that IPs and LCs-related projects received little ODF for biodiversity over 2011-2020 (OECD, 2023[16]), namely 4% on average of DAC member's total biodiversity-related ODF (although this figure is not directly comparable due to evolving methodologies). Importantly, 56% of the funding overlaps with activities addressing the priorities of the CBD as a main objective, underscoring the connections between IPs and LCs and nature.

Indeed, their inclusion is not just beneficial for their livelihoods but vital for the success and effectiveness of certain biodiversity-related projects. Recognising and integrating the unique knowledge and contributions of IPs and LCs, is key to achieving meaningful and lasting outcomes in biodiversity conservation, as well as supporting the right to free, prior, and informed consent (FPIC), co-operation and partnership. This is particularly highlighted in the United Nations Declaration on the Rights of Indigenous Peoples (UNDRIP) (UN, 2007[43]). For instance, Canada is working in partnership with First Nations, Inuit and Métis to guide Indigenous-led development co-operation programming (GAC, 2024[44]). This includes, for example, work under the Indigenous Peoples Partnering for Climate initiative, which supports Indigenous peoples climate resilience and leadership in implementing nature-based solutions for climate adaptation and biodiversity around the world (Government of Canada, 2024[45]).

Further, biodiversity ODF including IPs and LCs was targeted mainly to Peru, Ethiopia, Colombia, Burkina Faso, the Philippines, the Plurinational State of Bolivia, Kenya and Brazil (together accounting for 46% of the total without considering unspecified allocations). Overall, the most targeted regions were Africa (45%), followed by LAC (35%) and Asia (18%). About USD 266 million of total biodiversity-related development finance supporting IPs and LCs falls under the multi-regional or unspecified allocation categories (28% or 12%, respectively), yet still targets developing countries.

Canada and Norway targeted the largest overall share of their biodiversity-related ODF to IPs and LCs (45% and 23%, respectively), while Germany, Canada, the United States, Sweden and Norway were the largest contributors in absolute terms representing 71% of the total contributions. Other major donors included Switzerland, EU institutions, Spain and the United Kingdom. Overall, estimated biodiversity-related ODF supporting IPs and LCs was provided by standard grants (i.e. transfers with no legal debt incurred by the recipient). For example, Norway is helping to reduce deforestation in the Peruvian Amazon by strengthening Indigenous peoples' rights, promoting community forest management and actions to reduce illegal activities (Norad, 2024[46]). The support is channelled from the Norwegian government through Norway's International Climate and Forest Initiative to Peruvian government institutions through a dedicated financial mechanism for REDD+[2], as well as through international and Peruvian civil society organisations. In addition, Germany is supporting IPs and LCs to scale up conservation and the sustainable use of biodiversity by directly supporting local initiatives for self-determined land and resource governance, and the co-development of community-owned monitoring frameworks to present evidence and demonstrate outcomes (IKI, 2024[47]).

Importantly, the keywords listed in Table B.1 can vary in terms of specificity and a simple division of keywords would not allow for a well-founded classification to reflect a prioritisation of objectives, nor a distinction between activities encompassing IPs and LCs. Indeed, more information and resources would be needed to make correct estimations including, for example, checking filtered projects (goals, indicators, activities, actors) and looking into technical notes and monitoring and evaluation reports. As such, these estimates should be taken with caution when deriving statements on financing volumes. Moreover, information from the CRS allows seeing up to the first implementing partner of the project, posing thus a challenge to track the funding reaching IPs and LCs directly.

Biodiversity-related ODF related to IPs and LCs can target projects addressing a range of categories: capacity development, technology transfer and knowledge exchange; conflict, peace and security; energy; environment protection; finance and business development; governance; human rights; land and water tenure and resources rights; partnerships; policies and institutions; sustainable income and livelihoods; and, sustainable use and management of natural resources. Table B.2 provides an overview of the possible classification of environmental and IPs and LCs' activities according to the objectives and kind of activities pursued that could also be captured in OECD DAC statistics. Importantly, in most cases, projects are designed to deliver multi-purpose objectives, resulting in a combination of the different categories described. Further, the table also shows that the activities may also span across a range of sector and purpose codes based on the OECD DAC CRS, underscoring the cross-cutting characteristics of these activities.

In particular, some promising initiatives have been developed to support IPs and LCs, including by improving their participation on the use of natural resources, promoting their inclusion in decision making and the design of financial mechanisms, and increasing direct access to finance. The following initiatives showcase existing examples addressing these issues:

- The Global Environment Facility-funded Inclusive Conservation Initiative (ICI, 2024[48]), which aims to deploy USD 23 million and over USD 90 million of co-financing, to support the leadership of IPs and LCs in safeguarding nature and strengthening the capacity of Indigenous-led initiatives to conserve globally significant biodiversity and ecosystems.
- The World Bank recognises IP's critical role for ecosystems, climate mitigation and overall resilience. The Bank implements commitments through the Social Standard 7 (World Bank, 2016[49]) to ensure that Indigenous peoples can benefit from and be included in financial processes. It also established the Enhancing Access to Benefits while Lowering Emissions (EnABLE) multi-donor trust fund (World Bank, 2021[50]) to further support the inclusion of communities and contribute to improving the resilience of livelihoods, biodiversity conservation and climate change mitigation.

- The International Fund for Agricultural Development's Indigenous Peoples Assistance Facility (IPAF) (IFAD, 2024[51]) serves as an innovative funding instrument to strengthen Indigenous peoples' communities and their organisations through small grants projects that foster self-driven development. It is is managed by a board mostly composed of Indigenous peoples. Further, IPAF also helps implement the principles of engagement of IFAD's Policy on Indigenous Peoples (IFAD, 2022[52]).
- Australia has established an Ambassador for First Nations Peoples to ensure Indigenous representation in international engagement (DFAT, 2023[53]), seeking also to identify new areas of co-operation between First Nations communities and Australia's international partners, including development, climate change, intellectual property and trade, human rights, and tourism.

References

AECID (2022), *La Cooperación Española con la igualdad y los movimientos feminista y de mujeres de Honduras*, https://www.aecid.hn/sitio/index.php/menu-noticias-externo/865-la-cooperacion-espanola-con-la-igualdad-y-los-movimientos-feminista-y-de-mujeres-de-honduras (accessed on 8 July 2024). [37]

BIOFIN (2021), *The Biodiversity Finance Initiative*, https://www.biofin.org/. [14]

CBD (2024), *Introduction to the GBF: Section A. Background*, https://www.cbd.int/gbf/introduction (accessed on 9 July 2024). [33]

CBD (2022), *15/11. Gender Plan of Action. Decision adopted by the Conference of the Parties to the Convention on Biological Diversity*, Convention on Biological Diversity, https://www.cbd.int/doc/decisions/cop-15/cop-15-dec-11-en.pdf (accessed on 8 July 2024). [36]

CBD (2022), *Kunming-Montreal Global Biodiversity Framework*, https://www.cbd.int/doc/c/e6d3/cd1d/daf663719a03902a9b116c34/cop-15-l-25-en.pdf (accessed on 15 July 2024). [20]

CBD (n.d.), *Target 22: Ensure Participation in Decision-Making and Access to Justice and Information Related to Biodiversity for all*, https://www.cbd.int/gbf/targets/22 (accessed on 8 July 2024). [35]

CBD (n.d.), *Target 23: Ensure Gender Equality and a Gender-Responsive Approach for Biodiversity Action*, https://www.cbd.int/gbf/targets/23 (accessed on 8 July 2024). [34]

CBFP (2022), *Congo Basin Pledge*, https://pfbc-cbfp.org/congo-basin-pledge.html (accessed on 10 July 2024). [7]

CEPF (2024), *Explore the Biodiversity Hotspots*, https://www.cepf.net/our-work/biodiversity-hotspots (accessed on 19 November 2023). [15]

Cooperanda (2021), *Mejora de las capacidades productivas con base en la gestión sostenible del Manglar y el empoderamiento de mujeres y jóvenes en las comunidades de Macaneta, Gdzene, Macavule y Muntanhana en el distrito de Marracuene (Mozambique)*, https://cooperanda.org/explorar/proyectos/ver/mejora-de-las-capacidades-productivas-con-base-en-la-gestion-sostenible-del-manglar-y-el-empoderamiento-de-mujeres-y-jovenes-en-las-comunidades-de-macaneta-gdzene-macavule-y-muntanhana-en-el-distrit/ (accessed on 8 July 2024). [38]

Cooperanda (2019), *Metodología para la inclusión de la equidad de género en la implementación de la legislación relativa a la tenencia de la tierra en comunidades rurales de las provincias de Gaza y Maputo en Mozambique*, https://cooperanda.org/explorar/proyectos/ver/metodologia-para-la-inclusion-de-la-equidad-de-genero-en-la-implementacion-de-la-legislacion-relativa-a-la-tenencia-de-la-tierra-en-comunidades-rurales-de-las-provincias-de-gaza-y-maputo-en-mozambique/ (accessed on 8 July 2024). [39]

COP26 Presidency (2021), *COP26 IPLC forest tenure joint donor statement*, https://ukcop26.org/cop26-iplc-forest-tenure-joint-donor-statement/ (accessed on 31 January 2023). [4]

DFAT (2023), *Office for First Nations International Engagement/Ambassador for First Nations People*, https://www.dfat.gov.au/international-relations/themes/indigenous-peoples/ambassador-first-nations-people (accessed on 25 July 2024). [53]

FTFG (2023), *Indigenous Peoples and Local Communities Forest Tenure Pledge: Annual Report 2022–2023*, https://www.landportal.org/library/resources/indigenous-peoples-and-local-communities-forest-tenure-pledge (accessed on 10 July 2024). [5]

GAC (2024), *Statement on International Day of the World's Indigenous Peoples*, https://www.canada.ca/en/global-affairs/news/2024/08/statement-on-international-day-of-the-worlds-indigenous-peoples.html (accessed on 20 August 2024). [44]

GFFP (2023), *The Global Forest Finance Pledge - 2022 Progress Report*, https://forestclimateleaders.org/wp-content/uploads/2023/12/CCS0523480542-001_PN7164575_The-Global-Forest-Finance-Pledge-2022_Web-Accessible.pdf (accessed on 10 July 2024). [3]

GIZ (2024), *GBF Implementation: Strengthening National Implementation of Global Biodiversity Targets*, https://www.giz.de/en/downloads/giz2024-en-global-biodiversity-targets-implementation.pdf. [13]

Government of Canada (2024), *Partnering for Climate*, https://www.international.gc.ca/world-monde/funding-financement/partnering-climate-partenariats-climat.aspx?lang=eng (accessed on 20 August 2024). [45]

ICI (2024), *Enhancing Indigenous Peoples' and Local Communities' efforts to steward land, waters, and natural resources to deliver Global Environmental Benefits*, https://inclusiveconservationinitiative.org/ (accessed on 25 July 2024). [48]

IFAD (2024), *Indigenous Peoples Assistance Facility*, https://www.ifad.org/en/ipaf (accessed on 25 July 2024). [51]

IFAD (2022), *IFAD Policy on Engagement with Indigenous Peoples: 2022 update*, https://www.ifad.org/en/-/document/ifad-policy-on-engagement-with-indigenous-peoples (accessed on 25 July 2024). [52]

IKI (2024), *Transformative pathways: indigenous peoples and local communities leading and scaling up conservation and sustainable use of biodiversity*, https://www.international-climate-initiative.com/en/project/transformative-pathways-indigenous-peoples-and-local-communities-leading-and-scaling-up-conservation-and-sustainable-use-of-biodiversity-22-iv-108-global-a-iplcs-for-biodiversity/ (accessed on 25 July 2024). [47]

IPBES (2019), *Global assessment report on biodiversity and ecosystem services of the Intergovernmental Science-Policy Platform on Biodiversity and Ecosystem Services*, IPBES secretariat, https://doi.org/10.5281/zenodo.3831673. [17]

NBSAP Accelerator Partnership (2024), *Accelerating Action for Biodiversity*, https://nbsapaccelerator.org/ (accessed on 25 June 2024). [12]

Norad (2024), *Contribution to the Updated JDI Implementation Plan 2020-2025 and RENAMI: Profonanpe - Peruvian Trust Fund for National Parks and Protected Areas*, https://resultater.norad.no/avtale/PER-22/0005 (accessed on 25 July 2024). [46]

OECD (2024), *Climate Finance Provided and Mobilised by Developed Countries in 2013-2022*, Climate Finance and the USD 100 Billion Goal, OECD Publishing, Paris, https://doi.org/10.1787/19150727-en. [19]

OECD (2024), *Mainstreaming Biodiversity into Renewable Power Infrastructure*, OECD Publishing, Paris, https://doi.org/10.1787/357ac474-en. [31]

OECD (2024), *OECD DAC Creditor Reporting System Statistics*, OECD.Stat, https://data-explorer.oecd.org/s/c. [1]

OECD (2023), *A Decade of Development Finance for Biodiversity*, OECD Publishing, Paris, https://doi.org/10.1787/e6c182aa-en. [16]

OECD (2023), *Scaling Up the Mobilisation of Private Finance for Climate Action in Developing Countries: Challenges and Opportunities for International Providers*, Green Finance and Investment, OECD Publishing, Paris, https://doi.org/10.1787/17a88681-en. [9]

OECD (2019), "Decentralised development co-operation: Unlocking the potential of cities and regions", *OECD Development Policy Papers*, No. 22, OECD Publishing, Paris, https://doi.org/10.1787/e9703003-en. [8]

Parrotta, J. et al. (2022), "Forests, Climate, Biodiversity and People: Assessing a Decade of REDD+.", Vol. 40, p. 164. [27]

Pettorelli, N. et al. (2021), "Time to integrate global climate change and biodiversity science-policy agendas", *Journal of Applied Ecology*, https://doi.org/10.1111/1365-2664.13985 (accessed on 12 July 2024). [28]

PwC (2023), *Managing nature risks: From understanding to action*, Will Evison, Lit Ping Low, and Daniel O'Brien, https://www.pwc.com/gx/en/strategy-and-business/content/sbpwc-2023-04-19-Managing-nature-risks-v2.pdf (accessed on 7 July 2024). [23]

RFN (2021), *Falling short: Donor funding for Indigenous Peoples and local communities to secure tenure rights and manage forests in tropical countries (2011–2020)*, https://dv719tqmsuwvb.cloudfront.net/documents/Publikasjoner/Andre-rapporter/RFN_Falling_short_2021.pdf (accessed on 25 July 2024). [40]

Seddon, N. et al. (2021), "Getting the message right on nature-based solutions to climate change", *Global Change Biology*, Vol. 27/8, pp. 1518-1546, https://doi.org/10.1111/gcb.15513. [30]

UK COP26 (2021), *COP26 Congo Basin Joint Donor Statement: Supporting the protection and sustainable management of the Congo Basin forests*, https://webarchive.nationalarchives.gov.uk/ukgwa/20230106145223/https:/ukcop26.org/cop26-congo-basin-joint-donor-statement/ (accessed on 11 July 2024). [6]

UK COP26 (2021), *The Global Forest Finance Pledge: Financing the protection, restoration, and sustainable management of forests*, https://webarchive.nationalarchives.gov.uk/ukgwa/20230106145241/https://ukcop26.org/the-global-forest-finance-pledge/ (accessed on 10 July 2024). [2]

UN (2007), *United Nations Declaration on the Rights of Indigenous Peoples*, https://www.un.org/development/desa/indigenouspeoples/wp-content/uploads/sites/19/2018/11/UNDRIP_E_web.pdf (accessed on 20 August 2024). [43]

UNCCD (2022), *The Global Land Outlook, second edition*, https://www.unccd.int/sites/default/files/2022-04/UNCCD_GLO2_low-res_2.pdf (accessed on 9 July 2024). [26]

UNEP (2024), *6/4. Promoting synergies, cooperation or collaboration for national implementation of multilateral environmental agreements and other relevant environmental instruments*, https://daccess-ods.un.org/access.nsf/Get?OpenAgent&DS=UNEP/EA.6/RES.4&Lang=E (accessed on 9 July 2024). [32]

UNEP (2022), *UN Environment Assembly 5 (UNEA 5.2) Resolution 5: Nature-based solutions for supporting sustainable development*, https://wedocs.unep.org/bitstream/handle/20.500.11822/39864/NATURE-BASED%20SOLUTIONS%20FOR%20SUPPORTING%20SUSTAINABLE%20DEVELOPMENT.%20English.pdf?sequence=1&isAllowed=y (accessed on 31 July 2023). [29]

UNFCCC (2023), *Glasgow–Sharm el-Sheikh work programme on the global goal on adaptation referred to in decision 7/CMA.3*, https://unfccc.int/sites/default/files/resource/cma5_auv_8a_gga.pdf (accessed on 10 July 2024). [22]

UNFCCC (n.d.), *What is REDD+?*, https://unfccc.int/topics/land-use/workstreams/redd/what-is-redd (accessed on 4 September 2024). [54]

UNFCCC COP28 (2023), *COP28 Joint Statement on Climate, Nature and People*, https://www.cop28.com/en/joint-statement-on-climate-nature (accessed on 10 July 2024). [21]

UNPFII (2024), *United Nations Permanent Forum on Indigenous Issues: Report on the twenty-third session*, https://social.desa.un.org/sites/default/files/Webpage_Advance_Unedited-Version_UNPFII_2024_clean.pdf (accessed on 10 July 2024). [41]

UNPFII (2023), *United Nations Permanent Forum on Indigenous Issues: Report on the twenty-second session*, https://undocs.org/Home/Mobile?FinalSymbol=E%2F2023%2F43&Language=E&DeviceType=Desktop&LangRequested=False (accessed on 10 July 2024). [42]

USAID (2024), *USAID Tuhifadhi Maliasili ("Preserve Natural Resources")*, https://www.usaid.gov/tanzania/fact-sheet/tuhifadhi-maliasili-preserve-natural-resources (accessed on 1 July 2024). [10]

USAID (2022), *Forest 2018-2022: Stronger Forest Management Agencies and Greater Conservation of the Amazon*, https://pdf.usaid.gov/pdf_docs/PA00ZWMW.pdf (accessed on 1 July 2024). [11]

WEF (2024), *The Global Risks Report 2024*, https://www3.weforum.org/docs/WEF_The_Global_Risks_Report_2024.pdf (accessed on 15 July 2024). [25]

WEF (2020), *Nature Risk Rising: Why the Crisis Engulfing Nature Matters for Businesses and the Economy*, https://www3.weforum.org/docs/WEF_New_Nature_Economy_Report_2020.pdf (accessed on 15 July 2024). [18]

WEF (2020), *The Future Of Nature And Business. New Nature Economy project II*, In collaboration with AlphaBeta, https://www3.weforum.org/docs/WEF_The_Future_Of_Nature_And_Business_2020.pdf (accessed on 15 July 2024). [24]

World Bank (2021), *EnABLE - Enhancing Access to Benefits while Lowering Emissions*, https://www.worldbank.org/en/topic/climatechange/brief/enable-enhancing-access-to-benefits-while-lowering-emission (accessed on 25 July 2024). [50]

World Bank (2016), *World Bank Environmental and Social Framework*, https://thedocs.worldbank.org/en/doc/837721522762050108-0290022018/original/ESFFramework.pdf#page=89&zoom=80 (accessed on 25 July 2024). [49]

Notes

[1] The KMGBF acknowledges the "important roles and contributions of indigenous peoples and local communities as custodians of biodiversity and partners in the conservation, restoration and sustainable use" (CBD, 2022[20]). The term Indigenous peoples and local communities is used internationally to refer to individuals and communities who can be self-identified as Indigenous or as members of local communities that have a strong connection to place and nature through livelihoods, cultural identity, worldviews, institutions and ecological knowledge (IPBES, 2019[17]). Within this context, and acknowledging that the United Nations Declaration on the Rights of Indigenous Peoples recognises and respects the human rights of Indigenous peoples (UN, 2007[43]), the term is not intended to ignore differences and diversity within and among Indigenous peoples and between them and local communities. It is used largely to denote that there are communalities and shared concerns for Indigenous peoples and local communities, which are important in the context of development and biodiversity.

[2] REDD+: reducing emissions from deforestation and forest degradation in developing countries. The "+" stands for "conservation, sustainable management of forests and enhancement of forest carbon stocks" (UNFCCC, n.d.[54]).

4 Multilateral institutions' development finance for biodiversity

Looking at multilateral development finance for biodiversity (both concessional and non-concessional) using the biodiversity-related approach in Figure 4.1, estimates show an increase over 2015-22, from USD 1.4 billion in 2015 to USD 5.1 billion in 2021 and USD 11.3 billion in 2022, representing USD 4.8 billion on average for the period. Flows experienced a significant 123% increase from 2021 to 2022 (mainly explained by the significant-like activities). In relative terms, however, the estimated share of biodiversity-related development finance represents a low-share overall of total multilateral development finance over 2015-22 (3%) albeit increasing from 3% in 2021 to 6% in 2022. The peak share recorded in 2022 (6%) can be explained by the significantly high contributions from three multilateral development banks (MDBs, representing 65% of total biodiversity-related finance).

In addition, using the biodiversity-specific approach (see Box 2.1 and Annex A), the analysis finds (Figure 4.2) that finance provided by multilateral institutions increased from USD 0.6 billion in 2015 to USD 2.7 billion in 2021 and USD 5.7 billion in 2022, representing USD 2.4 billion for biodiversity activities on average over 2015-22 (representing 2% of total multilateral development finance). In this approach, contributions toward biodiversity-specific activities also increase by 115% from 2021 to 2022. Importantly, in both methodologies, although the share of principal-like biodiversity-related flows remains relatively small over the period (between 8% and 18% in 2015 to 18% to 36% in 2022), it has been increasing over time, almost doubling from 2021 to 2022, when it reached its peak volume (USD 2.1 billion).

Figure 4.1. Multilateral institutions' biodiversity-related development finance

2015-22, USD billion, full values

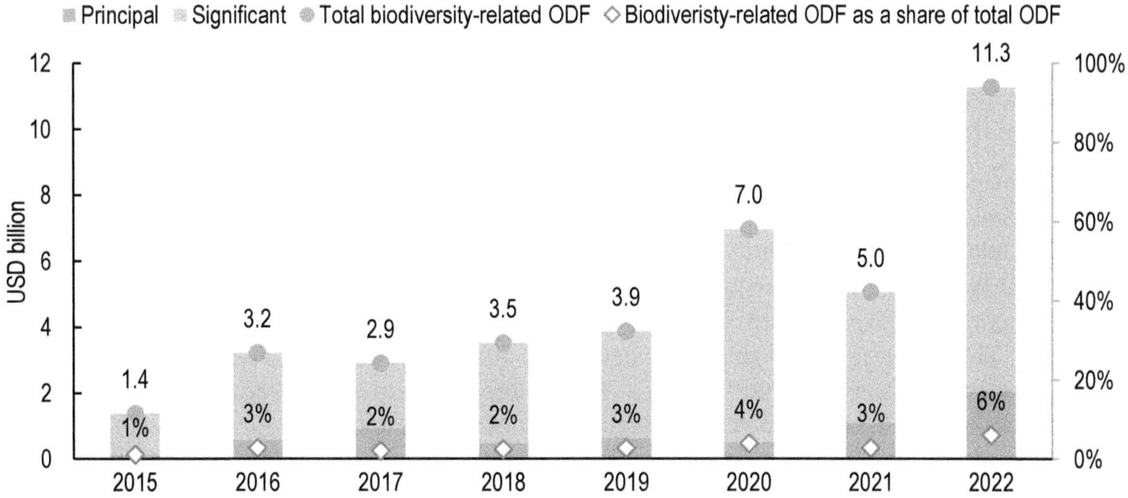

Notes: ODF: official development finance. The figure shows the full value of all multilateral flows reported to the OECD.
Sources: Authors' estimates based on OECD-DAC statistics from OECD (2024[1]), *Creditor Reporting System* (database), https://data-explorer.oecd.org/s/c and *Total Official Support for Sustainable Development* (database) from TOSSD (2024[2]), https://www.tossd.org.

Figure 4.2. Multilateral institutions' biodiversity-specific development finance

2015-22, USD billion, estimates with coefficients

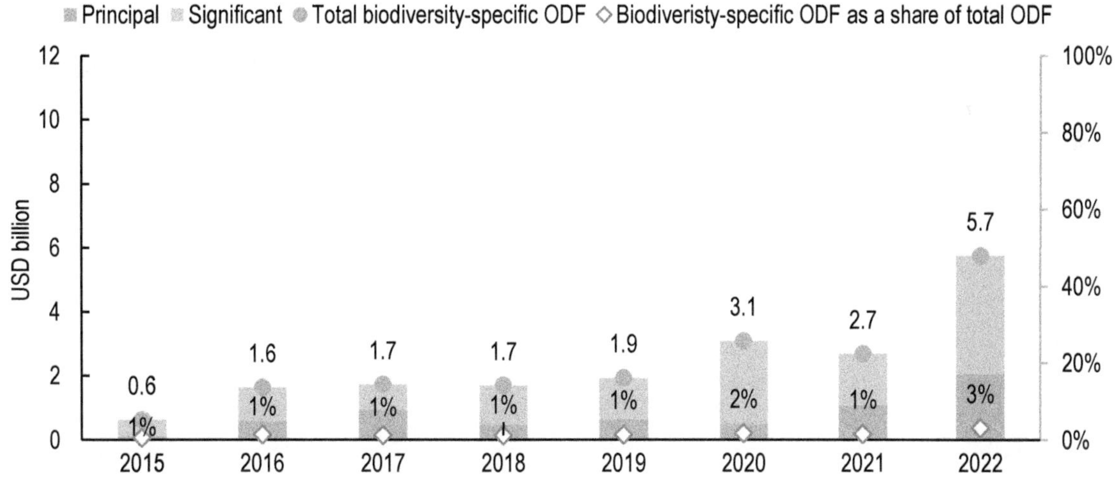

Notes: ODF: official development finance. The figure provides information on multilateral institutions' biodiversity-specific finance based on estimates with coefficients, reflecting the full value of their core (principal and "principal-like") activities and applying a coefficient for activities considered as secondary (significant and "significant-like"). Multilateral flows include principal, "principal-like", significant and "significant-like" data from a variety of sources, including Rio marker data on biodiversity, purpose code data, Sustainable Development Goals 14 and 15 data, and data captured through a keyword search (see Table A.1). For more information on the methodology used to obtain and analyse multilateral institutions' data, please consult Annex A. Commitments that were not classified by aid type or co-operation modalities were not included in this analysis.
Sources: Authors' estimates based on OECD-DAC statistics from OECD (2024[1]), *Creditor Reporting System* (database), https://data-explorer.oecd.org/s/c and *Total Official Support for Sustainable Development* (database) from TOSSD (2024[2]), https://www.tossd.org.

Almost all multilateral flows for biodiversity (92%) are provided by a few institutions, 9 out of the 65 included in the analysis, with the top 4 accounting for 61% of the total biodiversity-related finance (for a detailed list of institutions included see Annex A). MDBs accounted for 71% of total multilateral biodiversity-related development finance over 2015-22. In turn, other environmental funds and organisations that are part of the United Nations system account for 22% and 7%, respectively, of the total. Although in general total multilateral development finance was also provided by a few institutions over the period (92% reflected by 16 institutions, and the top four 53%), the composition varies by type, with 89% provided by MDBs, followed by 7% of other multilateral institutions and 4% by United Nations agencies.

Figure 4.3 provides an overview of the top ten recipients over 2015-22, which account for 52% of the total estimated development finance for biodiversity of multilateral institutions. In particular, the People's Republic of China (hereafter "China") received 17%, mainly provided by 3 MDBs (96%) through loans (97%), and targeting activities related to forest protection and restoration, ecological rehabilitation, sustainable agriculture development, and sustainable land-use management, including water resources conservation. Five of these top recipients coincide with the top bilateral biodiversity recipients, namely Colombia, Indonesia, Brazil, India and Ethiopia. The estimated share of biodiversity-related development finance accounts for 2-8% of total multilateral finance in these countries, except in China where it accounts for 14%. Biodiversity-related development finance accounts for a considerable share of total multilateral finance in Niue (42%), Malaysia (21%), Cuba (20%) and Fiji (19%). Most of the multilateral biodiversity-related development finance flows to upper middle-income countries (UMICs; 50%), followed by lower middle-income countries (LMICs; 26%), and least developed countries and other low-income countries (LDCs and LICs; 24%). Overall, although the top recipients tend to be concentrated around the same countries, these may also vary yearly and, recently, Côte d'Ivoire stands out as well, over 2021-22.

Figure 4.3. Top recipients of multilateral biodiversity-related development finance

2015-22, USD million, full values

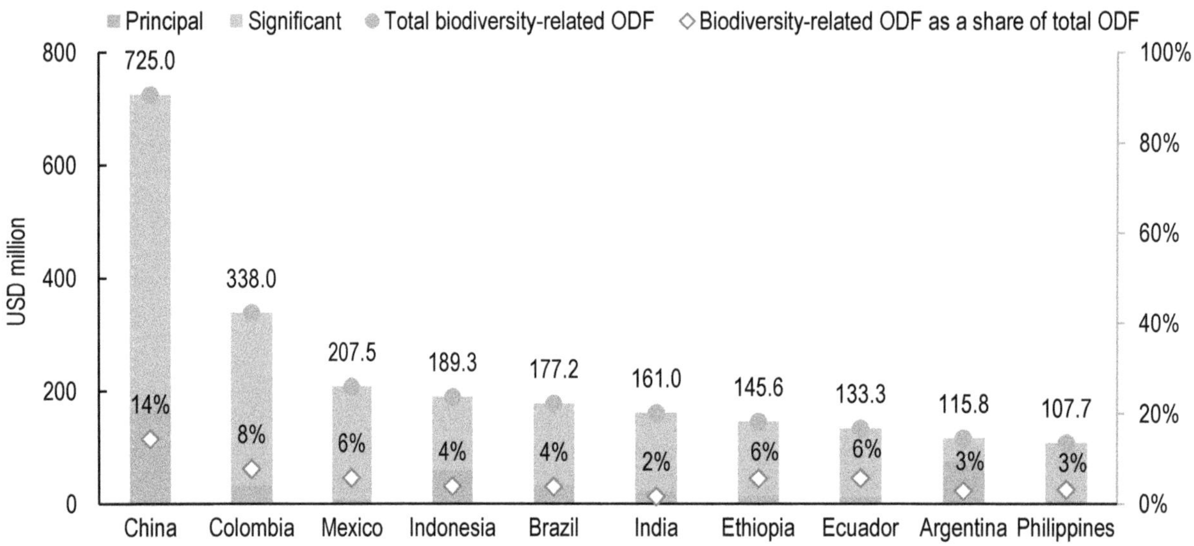

Notes: ODF: official development finance. The analysis excludes unspecified and regional allocations, which accounted for USD 185 million and USD 199 million, respectively, or 8% of total multilateral biodiversity-related development finance.
Sources: Authors' estimates based on OECD-DAC statistics from OECD (2024[1]), *Creditor Reporting System* (database), https://data-explorer.oecd.org/s/c and on *Total Official Support for Sustainable Development* (database) from TOSSD (2024[2]), https://www.tossd.org.

The region that received the most biodiversity-related development finance from multilateral institutions over 2015-22 was Asia with USD 1.8 billion (39%, of which 41% targets China only), followed by LAC with USD 1.5 billion (34%) and Africa with USD 1.14 billion (25%; Figure 4.4). In fact, Asia ranked up first on a yearly basis during this period, except in 2021 (i.e. second) and 2022 (i.e. third). Overall, these regions rank differently compared to the shares of total finance allocated during 2015-22: Asia (38%), Africa (31%) and LAC (23%). From an income-level perspective, the figures show that grants are predominantly used in LDCs and LICs (40%), and loans are predominantly used in MICs (57% and 27% in UMICs and LMICs, respectively). From a regional perspective, the estimates point at grants being mainly used in Africa (49% of total grants), while loans are mostly concentrated in Asia (45% of total loans). LAC receives relatively equal shares of all financial instruments being used yet predominantly attracts loans (37% of total loans). In addition, Oceania and Africa receive most of their funding through grants (57% and 52%, respectively), while Asia, LAC and Europe receive it through loans (84%, 81% and 72%, respectively).

Overall, multilateral biodiversity-related finance was mainly deployed through loans (70%) followed by grants (28%). This contrasts with how biodiversity-related development finance is provided by bilateral donors (which predominantly use grants), representing 68% of their flows over 2015-22, but reflects the mandates and operational environments of many of the multilateral institutions. In addition, while recognising their unique mandates, risk appetites, and financing modalities, several multilateral climate funds (e.g. Adaptation Fund, Climate Investments Funds, GEF and GCF) committed to jointly developing an Action Plan on Complementarity and Coherence (GCF, 2024[3]), aiming to increase access, harmonise efforts and enhance collaboration, having direct and indirect impacts on biodiversity finance.

Figure 4.4. Estimated biodiversity-related development finance from multilaterals by region

2015-22, USD, full values

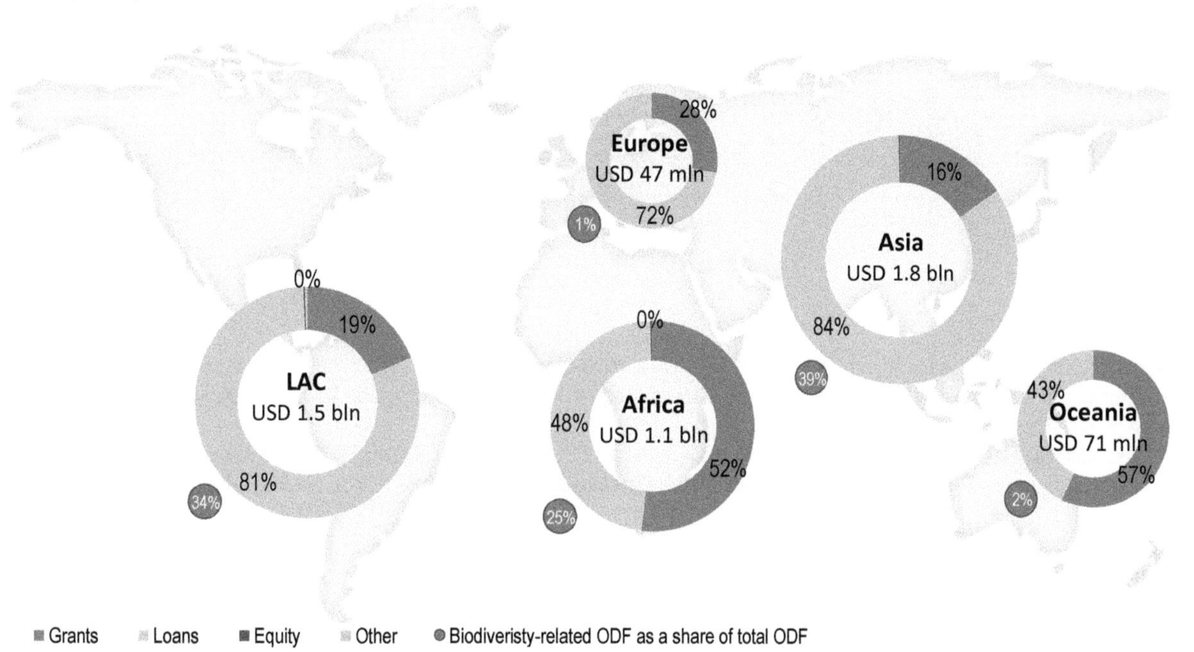

Notes: LAC: Latin America and the Caribbean; ODF: official development finance. Financial instruments represented include: grants (e.g. standard grants); debt instruments (e.g. standard loans, reimbursable grants and other debt securities); equity (e.g. common equity and shares in collective investment vehicles); and other instruments (e.g. subordinated loans and other hybrid instruments). 2. About 4% or USD 185 million of biodiversity-related ODF falls into the 'unallocated' category that is not earmarked to a country or region, and so has not been included into this analysis. 3. LAC = Latin America and the Caribbean.

Sources: Authors' estimates based on OECD-DAC statistics from OECD (2024[1]), *Creditor Reporting System* (database), https://data-explorer.oecd.org/s/c and *Total Official Support for Sustainable Development* (database) from TOSSD (2024[2]), https://www.tossd.org.

Most of the estimated multilateral biodiversity-related development finance is allocated to three sectors: 1) agriculture (22%); 2) general environment protection (16%); and 3) water (13%, including water supply and sanitation). This is similar to bilateral trends, which also prioritised agriculture (15%) or general environment protection (31%) when investing in biodiversity. In some sectors, the estimates show that biodiversity-related finance can be highly integrated into multilateral investments, notably in forestry (64%), general environment protection (50%, of which 41% was destined to biodiversity interventions) or fishing (37%; Figure 4.5). However, none of the sectors had biodiversity-related objectives as a main driver for multilateral investments (i.e. significant-like flows are higher than principal-like ones). In effect, multilateral institutions, and in particular MDBs, have committed to step up action to further mainstream nature into their policies and operations, as well as to develop methodologies to track and report "nature positive" investments (Box 4.1).

Figure 4.5. Top socio-economic areas receiving multilateral biodiversity-related development finance

2015-22, USD million, full values

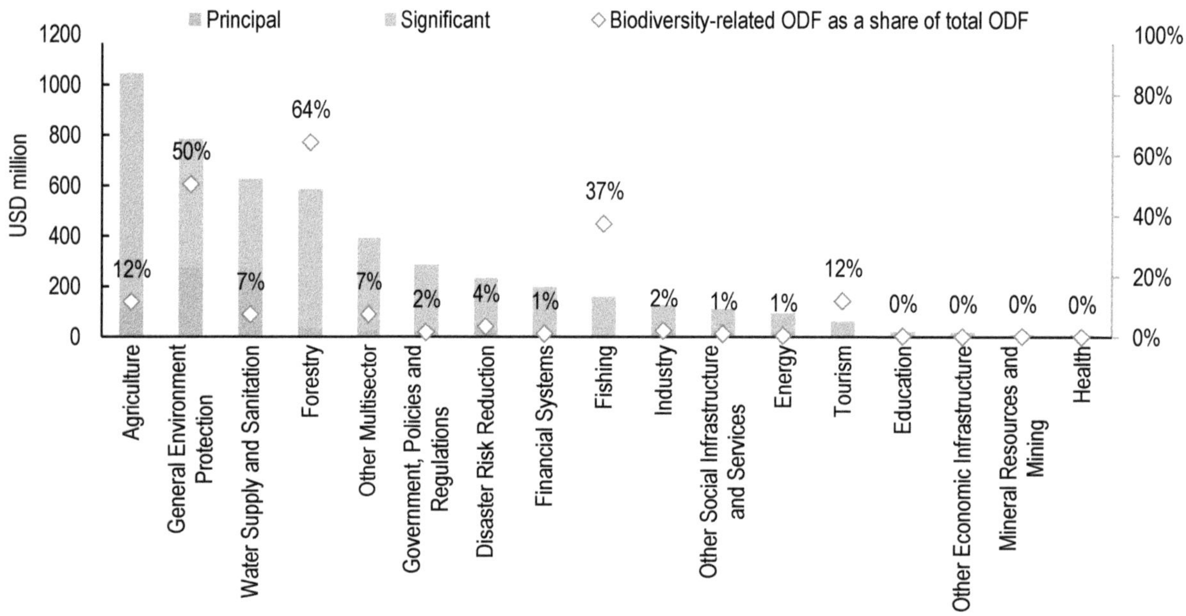

Notes: ODF: official development finance. About 0.2% or USD 10 million of biodiversity-related ODF falls into the "unallocated" category that is not earmarked to a sector, and so has not been included in this analysis. For further information on the classification of socio-economic areas please consult Annex B.

Sources: Authors' estimates based on OECD-DAC statistics from OECD (2024[1]), *Creditor Reporting System* (database), https://data-explorer.oecd.org/s/c and *Total Official Support for Sustainable Development* (database) from TOSSD (2024[2]), https://www.tossd.org.

Box 4.1. Tracking MDBs nature and biodiversity finance

In 2021, at the United Nations Framework Convention on Climate Change (UNFCCC) COP26, ten multilateral development banks (MDBs)[1] put forward a Joint MDB Statement on Nature, People and Planet (Multilateral Development Banks, 2021[4]), committing MDBs to further mainstream nature into their policies, investments and operations. In particular, MDBs committed to develop tools and methodologies to track and strengthen reporting on "nature-positive" investments, as well as to enhance public reporting on nature overall.

In line with this commitment, made on Nature Day of the UNFCCC COP28, MDBs defined a set of common principles to help identify, track and report nature-positive finance (MDBs, 2023[5]), facilitating the comparability across MDBs in their respective screening and tracking processes. As such, the common principles will help guide the development of MDBs' frameworks and internal methodologies for tracking nature-positive finance in a systemic manner while providing support to countries and the private sector in implementing the Kunming-Montreal Global Biodiversity Framework.

Indeed, nature action is gathering momentum among MDBs with further initiatives - including and beyond the focus on tracking investment volumes - ranging from the strengthening of biodiversity safeguards (ADB, 2023[6]), gathering and disclosure of data (EBRD, 2023[7]) and the establishment of partnerships (ADB, 2024[8]; EBRD, 2023[9]) to achieve synergies across actors. In particular, several MDBs (e.g. Asian Development Bank, European Bank for Reconstruction and Development, Inter-American Development Bank) have developed nature strategies, platforms and action plans (ADB, 2024[10]; IDB, 2024[11]; EBRD, 2023[12]) as additional steps to scaling up finance.

As MDBs work to address existing limitations regarding the quantification of biodiversity-related development finance, the OECD Secretariat has developed a specific methodology to identify multilateral biodiversity-related activities within the OECD *Creditor Reporting System* database, thus providing an estimate of multilateral development finance flows for biodiversity while ensuring the data captured are robust (see Annex A). Further, the G7 Foreign Ministers have called on MDBs to increase and report nature finance by CBD COP16 (FCDO, 2024[13]). The OECD looks forward to collaborating with the MDBs as they develop their taxonomy and methodologies to report on their efforts to support biodiversity-related activities, aligning the approaches, as suitable, as well as to engage with other institutions that have developed their own tracking methodology and are keen to align and avoid diverging efforts.

1. Asian Development Bank, African Development Bank Group, Asian Infrastructure Investment Bank, Caribbean Development Bank, European Bank for Reconstruction and Development, European Investment Bank, Inter-American Development Bank (IDB), IDB Invest, Islamic Development Bank, and the World Bank Group.

References

ADB (2024), *Canada and ADB Launch New Fund to Support Private Sector Climate Action and Nature-Based Solutions*, https://www.adb.org/news/canada-and-adb-launch-new-fund-support-private-sector-climate-action-and-nature-based (accessed on 30 August 2024). [8]

ADB (2024), *Nature Solutions Finance Hub for Climate and the Environment*, https://www.adb.org/publications/nature-solutions-finance-hub-climate-environment (accessed on 30 August 2024). [10]

ADB (2023), *Environmental and Social Framework (Consultation Draft)*, https://www.adb.org/documents/environmental-social-framework-draft (accessed on 30 August 2024). [6]

EBRD (2023), *Blue Mediterranean Partnership steps up support for sustainable blue economy*, https://www.ebrd.com/news/2023/blue-mediterranean-partnership-steps-up-support-for-sustainable-blue-economy.html (accessed on 30 August 2024). [9]

EBRD (2023), *Technical guidance for EBRD clients on uploading biodiversity data to the Global Biodiversity Information Facility*, https://eur02.safelinks.protection.outlook.com/?url=https%3A%2F%2Fwww.ebrd.com%2Fdocuments%2Fenvironment%2Ftechnical-guidance-for-ebrd-clients-on-uploading-biodiversity-data-to-the-global-biodiversity-information-facility-.pdf&data=05%7C02%7CDominique.BLA (accessed on 30 August 2024). [7]

EBRD (2023), *The EBRD Approach to Nature: Transitioning to a nature-positive economy*, https://www.ebrd.com/documents/environment/the-ebrds-approach-to-nature.pdf (accessed on 30 August 2024). [12]

FCDO (2024), *G7 Foreign Ministers' Meeting communiqué (Capri, 19 April 2024) – addressing global challenges, fostering partnerships*, https://www.gov.uk/government/publications/g7-foreign-ministers-meeting-communiques-april-2024/g7-foreign-ministers-meeting-communique-capri-19-april-2024-addressing-global-challenges-fostering-partnerships#:~:text=We%20reiterate%20the%20need%20to,terrori (accessed on 7 July 2024). [13]

GCF (2024), *Enhancing coherence and complementarity. Annex II. The Multilateral Climate Funds Action Plan on Complementarity and Coherence*, https://www.greenclimate.fund/sites/default/files/document/15-enhancing-coherence-and-complementarity-gcf-b39-11.pdf (accessed on 22 August 2024). [3]

IDB (2024), *IDB Group Launches Action Plan to Accelerate Natural Capital and Biodiversity Inclusion in Development Projects*, https://www.iadb.org/en/news/idb-group-launches-action-plan-accelerate-natural-capital-and-biodiversity-inclusion (accessed on 30 August 2024). [11]

MDBs (2023), *MDB Common Principles for tracking nature-positive finance*, https://www.eib.org/attachments/lucalli/20230329_mdb_common_principles_for_tracking_nature_positive_finance_en.pdf (accessed on 22 May 2024). [5]

Multilateral Development Banks (2021), *Joint Statement by the Multilateral Development Banks: Nature, People and Planet*, http://Joint Statement by the Multilateral Development Banks: Nature, People and Planet. [4]

OECD (2024), *OECD DAC Creditor Reporting System Statistics*, OECD.Stat, https://data-explorer.oecd.org/s/c. [1]

TOSSD (2024), *Total Official Support for Sustainable Development*, https://www.tossd.org/. [2]

5 South-South and triangular co-operation and other bilateral providers and biodiversity

Funding for biodiversity-related activities from bilateral providers beyond the Development Assistance Committee (DAC) membership, including South-South and triangular co-operation ("South-South") providers, amounted to USD 28 million annually on average over 2018-22, the years when most information on these providers is included in the OECD database. These volumes are driven mainly by Saudi Arabia, the United Arab Emirates, Brazil and Kazakhstan [which report to the *Creditor Reporting System* (CRS) and/or *Total Official Support for Sustainable Development* (TOSSD)]. Data available over these years indicate that contributions fluctuated over this period, from USD 40.2 million in 2018 to USD 26.9 million in 2021 and USD 30 million in 2022, increasing by 11% in 2022 compared to 2021 (Figure 5.1), and mostly targeting activities related to general environmental protection (38%) and agriculture (31%), followed by fishing (9%) and government, policies and regulations (8%).

It is important to highlight that not all providers of South-South co-operation report to the CRS or TOSSD [e.g. Argentina, the People's Republic of China (hereafter "China"), Colombia, India or South Africa]. This lack of reporting indicates a data gap, suggesting that the figures currently available likely underestimate the contributions to biodiversity-related development finance.

Overall, in terms of regional co-operation, most financing was directed to Africa (62%), followed by Asia (31%) then Latin America and the Caribbean (LAC; 5%) over 2018-22. The top 10 recipients account for 87% of the total estimated development finance for biodiversity (of which 37% is allocated to Egypt and 18% to China). Of these, only China and Ethiopia overlap with the main recipients of DAC and multilateral providers, highlighting the complementary role and distinctive geographical outreach of these players.

Figure 5.1. Development finance for biodiversity from bilateral providers beyond the DAC

2015-22, USD million, full values

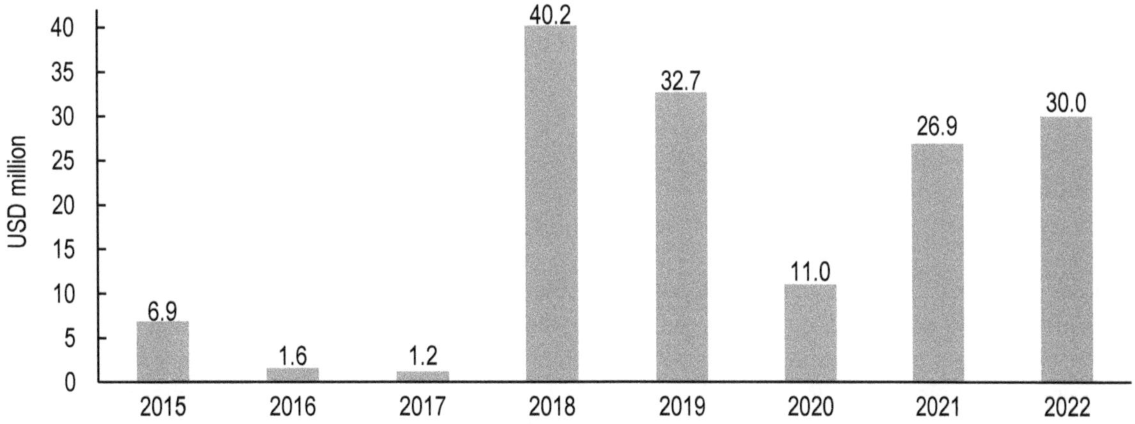

Notes: Non-DAC countries include Azerbaijan, Bulgaria, Croatia, Cyprus, Estonia (until 2020 inclusive), Israel, Kazakhstan, Kuwait, Latvia, Liechtenstein, Lithuania (until 2022), Malta, Monaco, Qatar, Romania, Saudi Arabia, Thailand, Türkiye and the United Arab Emirates. These flows are recorded in the *Creditor Reporting System*. South-South and triangular co-operation providers (South-South) include Brazil, Chile, Costa Rica, the Dominican Republic, Ecuador, Indonesia, Kazakhstan, Mexico and Peru, whose flows were reported through the TOSSD framework. Given that some countries report to both the CRS and TOSSD databases, attention was paid to avoid double counting.
Source: Authors' estimates based on OECD-DAC statistics from OECD (2024[1]), *Creditor Reporting System* (database), https://data-explorer.oecd.org/s/c and on *Total Official Support for Sustainable Development* (database) from TOSSD (2024[2]), https://www.tossd.org.

In addition, most contributions were implemented through public sector institutions (64%) both from provider governments (e.g. ministries of agriculture, fisheries, environment and natural resources, and international development co-operation agencies) and recipient governments (e.g. central governments, municipalities, public schools and universities), followed by multilateral organisations (20%, of which 40% corresponds to United Nations agencies, funds or commissions), and non-governmental organisations and civil society (10%) (e.g. Sahara Conservation Fund, Southern Alliance for Indigenous Resources, ECOTOP Foundation, Aves Argentina, International Union for the Conservation of Nature).

Moreover, some providers also have specific agencies dedicated to preserving natural heritage and protecting species, such as the United Arab Emirate's Mohamed bin Zayed Species Conservation Fund (Mohamed bin Zayed Species Conservation Fund, 2024[3]) that provides small grants (maximum of USD 25 000 per project) for individual species conservation initiatives (e.g. for black-faced lion, golden-bellied mangabey, Indochinese flying squirrel, Sunda pangolin, Wolkberg Zulu). Another example concerns Saudi Arabia where the Saudi Fund for Development focuses on preserving the environment and public health, such as finance provided to China for the environmental protection and sustainable development of wetlands around Hwange Lake (SFD, 2022[4]).

It is important to note that South-South co-operation, which inherently aims to strengthen capacities and address common problems among partners, also plays a crucial and complementary role to financial assistance by exchanging good practices and technical knowledge, providing technical assistance, and enhancing capacity development, based on a shared vision on principles and values about common goals, prioritising people and the planet. As such, many of their contributions are not necessarily reflected in monetary terms yet contribute greatly to the promotion of practices to reduce biodiversity loss and strengthen the sustainable use of natural resources. For example, Mexico and Peru are contributing to the development of forest monitoring systems through the exchange of technical knowledge, experiences and good practices based on forest inventories and satellite systems (APCI, 2021[5]) while Chile is exchanging experiences and knowledge regarding mineral extractive systems with Argentina to support Argentina in understanding control processes and the use of environmental management plans, as well as the negative impacts from open-pit mining and how to overcome them (AGCID, 2021[6]). Brazil is co-operating with Senegal by exchanging experiences and challenges on agroecological production – including pest and disease controls and water management – as well as on technical knowledge and training regarding organic certification and market development (ABC, 2019[7]). Other initiatives may also involve the development of alliances or the participation of several partners, as is the case of triangular co-operation initiatives (Box 5.1).

Box 5.1. The potential of triangular co-operation to address environmental issues

Triangular co-operation reflects the participation of different stakeholders (e.g. countries, international organisations, civil society, the private sector, private philanthropy) working together to address common challenges such as the Sustainable Development Goals (SDGs), biodiversity loss, climate change and ocean protection. In terms of implementation, triangular initiatives can be characterised by a facilitating partner that provides financial and technical support, while at least two other partners provide know-how and capacity development in support of a partner that seeks to tackle a specific development challenge. An example of this is the exchange of experiences among Costa Rica, the Dominican Republic and Honduras to strengthen and create structures and public policies dedicated to the management, conservation and restoration of coral reefs (e.g. gardening, nurseries and micro-fragmentation techniques) in which Germany, through GIZ's Regional Fund for Triangular Cooperation in Latin America and the Caribbean is the facilitating partner (GIZ, 2022[8]), and Costa Rica and the Dominican Republic serve as pivotal partners to support Honduras (Estrategia Nacional de Biodiversidad, 2019[9]).

Indeed, triangular co-operation demonstrates significant potential to address environmental issues, particularly when integrated with decentralised co-operation (SEGIB, 2023[10]). This integration can be important given the specific characteristics of the environmental sector and its local impacts, which may require the strengthening of multiple stakeholders and alliances. In particular, triangular co-operation initiatives for biodiversity in Ibero-America have been increasing through time, and the protection and conservation of the environment is the sector with the highest priority within this modality (SEGIB, 2023[11]). The prominence of environmental initiatives in triangular co-operation underscores its potential and reflects its underlying principles to address shared problems.

At the Second High-level United Nations Conference on South-South Co-operation held in Buenos Aires, Argentina, in 2019 (i.e. BAPA +40), the global development community reiterated its commitment to promote South-South and triangular co-operation as a means to achieve the 2030 Agenda for Sustainable Development (UN, 2019[12]), recognising the need to foster horizontal partnerships, co-create solutions, share knowledge and expertise, and scale up resources. Indeed, the upcoming International Meeting on Triangular Co-operation to be held in October 2024 in Lisbon can provide an opportunity to raise awareness on the need to protect our environment and promote the sustainable use and management of natural resources, and how triangular co-operation can best support this.

In addition, *Total Official Support for Sustainable Development* (TOSSD) is working to reflect the engagement of different stakeholders in triangular co-operation. TOSSD collects data on this framework of collaboration: for 2022, TOSSD collected triangular co-operation activities from 22 providers, including traditional and South-South co-operation providers, as well as international organisations. The International Forum on TOSSD also showcases triangular co-operation data through infographics and data stories (e.g. in the Philippines, SDG 15 concentrated most of the South-South and triangular co-operation flows) (TOSSD, 2022[13]).

References

ABC (2019), *Especialistas senegaleses conhecem práticas agroecológicas no Brasil*, https://www.gov.br/abc/pt-br/assuntos/noticias/especialistas-senegaleses-conhecem-praticas-agroecologicas-no-brasil (accessed on 3 July 2024). [7]

AGCID (2021), *Resolucion de Proyecto de Cooperacion Descentralizada: "Transferencia de conocimientos en procesos de control y fiscalización minera de yacimientos metalíferos, para ser aplicados en la Región de La Puna, en la Provincia de Salta"*, https://www.agci.cl/gobiernotransparente/documentos/Res_ex_237_2021.pdf (accessed on 15 July 2024). [6]

APCI (2021), *Situación y Tendencias de la Cooperación Técnica Internacional en el Perú 2021*, https://perusostenible.org/wp-content/uploads/2023/04/Situacio%CC%81n-y-Tendencias-de-la-Cooperacio%CC%81n-Te%CC%81cnica-Internacional-en-el-Peru%CC%81-2021.pdf. [5]

Estrategia Nacional de Biodiversidad (2019), *Aplicación de herramientas innovadoras para la conservación y restauración de arrecifes de coral en Honduras. Propuesta de proyecto Fondo Regional para la Cooperación Triangular en América Latina y el Caribe*, https://enbcr.go.cr/sites/default/files/verificador_m15_proyecto_triangular_.pdf (accessed on 1 July 2024). [9]

GIZ (2022), *Regional Fund for Triangular Cooperation in Latin America and the Caribbean*, https://www.giz.de/en/worldwide/12942.html (accessed on 17 June 2024). [8]

Mohamed bin Zayed Species Conservation Fund (2024), *Mohamed bin Zayed Species Conservation Fund*, https://www.speciesconservation.org/ (accessed on 17 June 2024). [3]

OECD (2024), *OECD DAC Creditor Reporting System Statistics*, OECD.Stat, https://data-explorer.oecd.org/s/c. [1]

SEGIB (2023), *Informe de la Cooperación Sur-Sur y Triangular en Iberoamérica 2022*, https://informesursur.org/es/report/informe-de-la-cooperacion-sur-sur-y-triangular-en-iberoamerica-2022/ (accessed on 20 August 2024). [11]

SEGIB (2023), *Una Cooperación Triangular innovadora para una nueva Agenda de Desarrollo*, Secretaría General Iberoamericana, https://www.segib.org/wp-content/uploads/Publicacion-Final-CT_ESP-V9-7-2-2023-web_Es.pdf (accessed on 25 July 2024). [10]

SFD (2022), *Annual Report 2022*, https://www.sfd.gov.sa/sites/default/files/annual-report-pdfs/AnnualReport_2022_EN.pdf (accessed on 15 July 2024). [4]

TOSSD (2024), *Total Official Support for Sustainable Development*, https://www.tossd.org/. [2]

TOSSD (2022), *More than 4500 South-South co-operation activities in TOSSD. What do the data tell us?*, https://www.tossd.org/pilot-studies-data-stories/tossd-south-south-cooperation.htm (accessed on 24 June 2024). [13]

UN (2019), *Buenos Aires outcome document of the second High-level United Nations Conference on South-South Cooperation*, https://www.unsouthsouth.org/wp-content/uploads/2019/10/N1911172.pdf (accessed on 10 July 2024). [12]

6 Private philanthropies and biodiversity

Grant-making by private philanthropic foundations in support of biodiversity-related areas is increasing. In 2017, philanthropies provided USD 501 million, while it was almost USD 1 billion in 2021. In 2022, however, philanthropic grants for biodiversity goals fell back to USD 700 million, which was still an increase of 40% compared to 2017 (Figure 6.1). Overall, private philanthropies provided USD 665 million on average over 2017-22 and are important actors in sectors such as general environment protection, including biodiversity conservation, agriculture and fishing (60%, 13% and 9% of their total contributions to biodiversity, respectively).

Figure 6.1. Biodiversity-related finance by private philanthropy

2015-22, USD million, full values

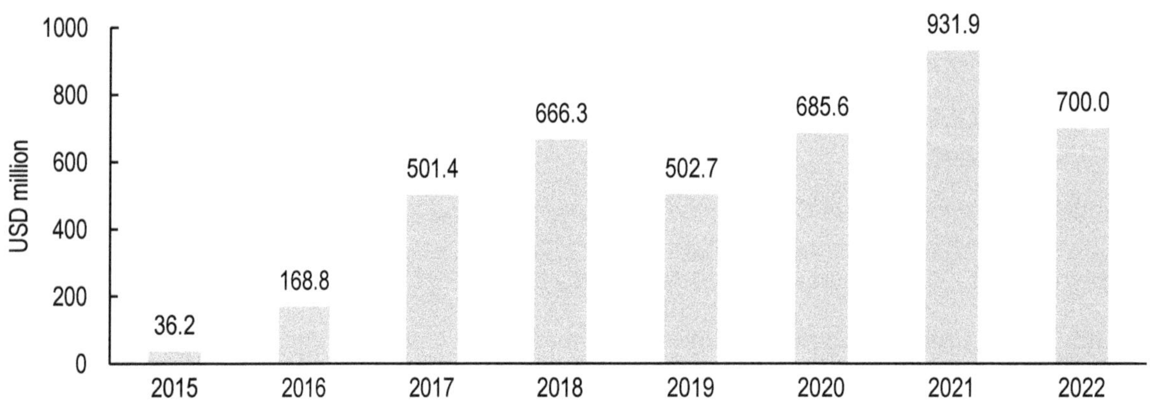

Note: Out of the 47 foundations that have been reporting to the OECD, 40 supported biodiversity-related activities.
Source: Authors' estimates based on OECD-DAC statistics from OECD (2024[1]), *Creditor Reporting System* (database), https://data-explorer.oecd.org/s/c.

The origin of philanthropic contributions for biodiversity is highly concentrated. Of the 40 foundations included in the OECD database that reported on biodiversity-related activities, Bezos Earth Fund, the Postcode Lottery Group, Gordon and Betty Moore Foundation, and the David and Lucile Packard Foundation were the most significant donors, providing 51% of the total biodiversity-related philanthropic giving over the period 2017-22, while 81% was provided by only 10 foundations (Figure 6.2).

In relative terms, Gordon and Betty Moore Foundation, the MAVA Foundation and the Arcadia Fund show the strongest focus on biodiversity, allocating more than two-thirds of their annual grant-making to the conservation of nature and related aspects. Box 6.1 provides an overview of private philanthropy in the context of development and biodiversity, exploring the overall coverage of biodiversity-related philanthropic flows and highlighting the gaps (and opportunities) towards a fuller philanthropic picture for biodiversity.

Figure 6.2. Top foundations of biodiversity-related international finance

2017-22 annual average, USD million, full values

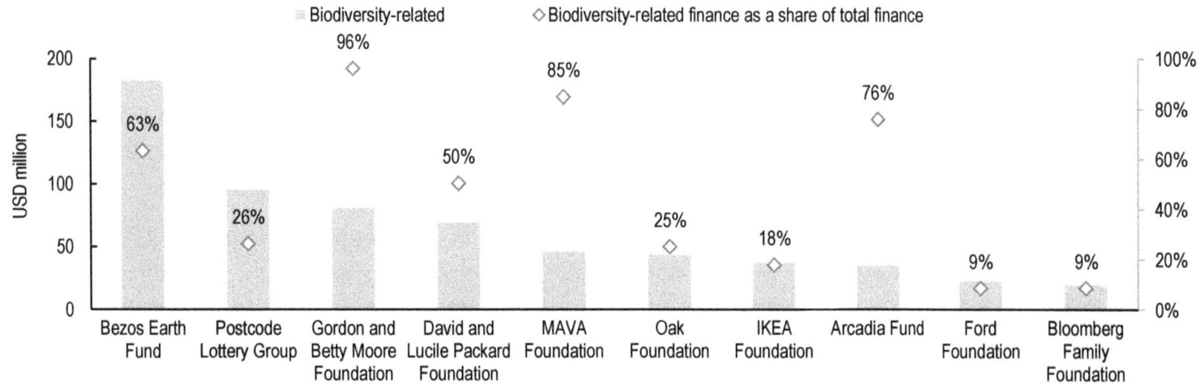

Notes: Finance provided by Bezos Earth Fund was based on 2020-22 due to data availability. Going forward, the analysis will take into consideration the MAVA Foundation's closure in 2022. The Postcode Lottery Group reflects contributions from the Dutch Postcode Lottery, German Postcode Lottery, Norwegian Postcode Lottery, People's Postcode Lottery and the Swedish Postcode Lottery.
Source: Authors' estimates based on OECD-DAC statistics from OECD (2024[1]), *Creditor Reporting System* (database), https://data-explorer.oecd.org/s/c.

Box 6.1. Coverage of biodiversity-related philanthropic flows and missing amounts

Private philanthropies play an important role in the context of development and biodiversity. This is reflected, for example, by their increasing participation in the Conferences of the Parties (COPs) of the Rio Conventions and engagement in international fora, as well as through their commitments [e.g. Protecting Our Planet Challenge (POP, n.d.[2]), Climate and Land Use Alliance (Climate and Land Use Alliance, 2024[3]), IPLC Forest Tenure Pledge (Land Portal, 2023[4])]. Thanks to their flexible mission statements and funding models, contributions made by private philanthropies can be unique and largely complementary to those made by other stakeholders. Using their networks and access to local and international actors, they can leverage their comparative advantage to promote innovation for greater impact. They can also support novel approaches that can mobilise commercial capital, whether through providing seed capital or de-risking other actors' investments (e.g. they can absorb first losses in collective investment vehicles or enterprises).

To promote transparency of development finance and evidence-based policies, 47 of the largest private philanthropic foundations have been reporting their data on development-related grants and programme/mission-related investments to the OECD. While the coverage of this dataset could be considered comprehensive, it is hard to provide an evidence-based estimation of data gaps due to a lack of alternative sources. Still, the following non-reporting philanthropies are known to provide resources for the conservation of nature in developing countries, with annual giving combined fluctuating at around USD 100 million:

- **Marisla Foundation**. Out of its annual grant making for biodiversity, approximately USD 10-15 million is estimated to be allocated to developing countries.
- **Rob Walton Foundation**. Working with renowned international conservation organisations, the foundation provided over USD 30 million in 2022, most notably to the African Parks Foundation for the rehabilitation and long-term management of protected areas in Africa.

- **Walton Family Foundation**. As part of its priority funding areas, the foundation promotes biodiversity conservation and sustainable fishing practices and other nature-related causes in developing countries. In 2018, its grant making for nature conservation in developing countries exceeded USD 30 million.
- **Wyss Foundation**. Working to preserve nature across the world, the foundation is estimated to have given more than USD 50 million for projects in developing countries in 2022. For example, during that year, it provided a USD 14.3 million grant to the African Parks Foundation to protect natural habitats on behalf of local governments and USD 11.5 million to the Andes Amazon Fund to permanently protect threatened and important intact forests.

Overall, continued efforts are needed to build transparency in this area and foster visibility in the contributions of all stakeholders in the domain of biodiversity conservation, including private philanthropic foundations. The availability of ready-to-use evidence is key to learning, setting multi-stakeholder collaboratives, and designing effective policies for the people and nature.

Source: Authors' research.

Philanthropic foundations mostly provided biodiversity-related funding to middle-income countries (78% of the philanthropy total), such as Indonesia, Brazil, India, Kenya, India, Peru and Colombia (together accounting for 44% of the total without considering unspecified allocations). The remaining 22% of the country-allocable funding targeted least developed countries, such as the Democratic Republic of the Congo, Rwanda, and Ethiopia. Overall, the most targeted regions were Africa (42%) followed by Latin America and the Caribbean (33%) and Asia (22%). About USD 429 million of total biodiversity-related finance falls under the multi-regional or unspecified allocation categories (15% or 49%, respectively), yet still targets developing countries.

In addition, almost all philanthropic contributions (76%) were implemented through non-governmental organisations (NGOs) and civil society and international NGOs in particular (such as the Worldwide Wildlife Fund, ClimateWorks Foundation, The Nature Conservancy, Rockefeller Philanthropy Advisors, or Fauna and Flora International), followed by academia or research institutes (13%). Public-private partnerships and networks were also used to deliver investments towards biodiversity-related contributions (5%). For instance, Gordon and Betty Moore Foundation has worked with the World Economic Forum to support the Tropical Forest Alliance in its efforts to advance deforestation and conservation-free commitments and commodities through private sector leadership and policy reform in South America (i.e. Argentina, Brazil and Paraguay) (Moore, 2022[5]). Another example is the MAVA Foundation's small grants programme in the Balkans (e.g. Albania, Bosnia and Herzegovina and North Macedonia) to support partners' capacities (e.g. Critical Ecosystem Partnership Fund) and promote ecosystem restoration and biodiversity conservation. In particular, from 2016 to 2022 (MAVA's closure), the MAVA Foundation focused on investing in strategic partnerships (MAVA & FOS, 2021[6]), by connecting projects and partners, to ensure the sustainability of conservation actions.

Private philanthropies are also helping to strengthen habitat protection, ecological connectivity and public recreation, through land acquisition, easements and facilitating wildlife movement, further helping countries to achieve Target 3 of the Kunming-Montreal Global Biodiversity Framework of protecting at least 30% of global land and ocean by 2030 (the 30X30 target) (CBD, 2022[7]). For instance, Gordon and Betty Moore Foundation has provided a grant to establish the Global Conservation Fund, designed to create and expand protected areas – e.g. national parks, privately-owned lands, community-managed reserves – and combining conservation with responsible nature use and development while helping to establish sustainable financing mechanisms to create a steady flow of funds for their effective management (Conservation International, 2023[8]). In collaboration with Conservation International and a global network of about 80 partners across at least 45 countries, until the Global Conservation Fund initiative ended, it had helped create or expand 135 protected areas, leveraging USD 259 million in funds from partners, creating jobs and helping to conserve the habitat of globally threatened species (GEF, 2017[9]). In addition, the Bezos Earth Fund, through coalitions of NGOs, governments and local partners, is also supporting initiatives to deliver the 30X30 target by helping to create, expand and strengthen the management of protected areas (Bezos Earth Fund, 2024[10]). For example, the fund has partnered with Re:Wild to support the establishment of a transnational marine protected area, including waters of Colombia, Costa Rica, Ecuador and Panama (Bezos Earth Fund, 2022[11]), as well as partnering with the Jane Goodall Institute with the aim of creating and reinforcing new community-managed protected areas in the Democratic Republic of Congo and the Republic of Congo, while supporting the preservation of cultural integrity and environmental value of the Congo Basin rainforest (Bezos Earth Fund, 2023[12]).

References

Bezos Earth Fund (2024), *Protecting 30% of the Planet by 2030*, https://www.bezosearthfund.org/ideas/protecting-30-of-the-planet-by-2030 (accessed on 15 July 2024). [10]

Bezos Earth Fund (2023), *Scaling Protected Areas in the Democratic Republic of Congo and the Republic of Congo*, https://www.bezosearthfund.org/grants/scaling-protected-areas-congo-basin-jane-goodall-institute (accessed on 15 July 2024). [12]

Bezos Earth Fund (2022), *Creating the Largest Multi-country Marine Protected Area in the World*, https://www.bezosearthfund.org/grants/creating-largest-multicountry-marine-protected-area-world (accessed on 15 July 2024). [11]

CBD (2022), *Target 3: Conserve 30% of Land, Waters and Seas*, https://www.cbd.int/gbf/targets/3 (accessed on 15 July 2024). [7]

Climate and Land Use Alliance (2024), *Climate and Land Use Alliance*, https://www.climateandlandusealliance.org/. [3]

Conservation International (2023), *Global Conservation Fund: Ensuring the permanent protection of the natural areas most essential to human well-being through innovative financing solutions*, https://www.conservation.org/about/global-conservation-fund (accessed on 15 July 2024). [8]

GEF (2017), *Global Conservation Fund: World-Changing Impacts, 2001-2016*, https://www.thegef.org/sites/default/files/publications/GCF%20Moore%20Report%20Exec%20Summary_FINAL4-17.pdf (accessed on 15 July 2024). [9]

Land Portal (2023), *Donor Pledge to Advance Indigenous Peoples' and Local Communities' Tenure Rights and their Forest Guardianship*, https://landportal.org/iplc/forest-tenure-donor-pledge. [4]

MAVA & FOS (2021), *Strategic Partnerships: MAVA's approach to scaling up conservation impact*, https://mava-foundation.org/wp-content/uploads/2023/02/mava_strategic_partnerships_booksprint-010721-1..pdf (accessed on 4 March 2024). [6]

Moore (2022), *Gordon and Betty Moore Foundation*, https://www.moore.org/grant-detail?grantId=GBMF11074 (accessed on 4 March 2024). [5]

OECD (2024), *OECD DAC Creditor Reporting System Statistics*, OECD.Stat, https://data-explorer.oecd.org/s/c. [1]

POP (n.d.), *Protecting Our Planet Challenge*, https://www.protectingourplanetchallenge.org/. [2]

7 Private finance mobilisation for biodiversity

Mobilising private sector finance is essential to deliver on the Kunming-Montreal Global Biodiversity Framework's targets (CBD, 2022[1]). According to the latest data (OECD, 2024[2]), private finance mobilised by official providers for biodiversity more than doubled between 2021 and 2022, up from USD 749 million in 2021 to USD 1.8 billion in 2022 (Figure 7.1). Over 2017-22, financing in this space mainly targeted activities related to water resources conservation, core biodiversity-related activities (e.g. conservation and protection of wetlands, endangered species and natural reserves) and biosphere protection (e.g. air and marine pollution control), financial and environmental policy and administrative management, small and medium-sized enterprises and business development, energy generation from renewable sources, and agricultural and forestry development (e.g. agricultural financial services, alternative development, water and land resources, crop production).

Figure 7.1. Mobilisation of private finance for biodiversity

2016-22, USD million, full values

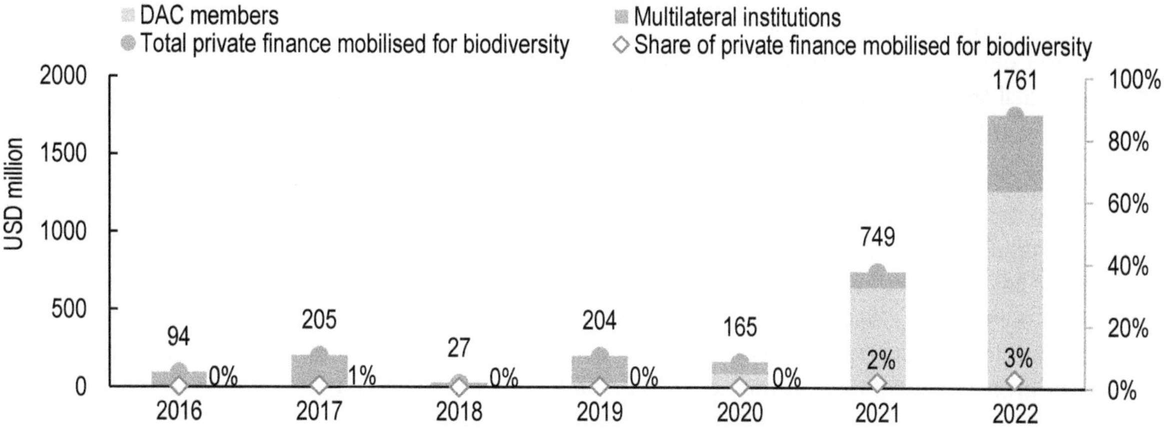

Notes: DAC: Development Assistance Committee; ODF: official development finance. The analysis only captures 2017-22 data given that data on biodiversity prior to this range are limited, mainly due to evolving methodologies and quality of data reporting. For more information, see Annex A.
Source: Authors' estimates based on OECD-DAC statistics from OECD (2024[3]), *Creditor Reporting System* (database), on mobilised private finance from OECD (2024[2]), http://data-explorer.oecd.org/s/q.

Although increasing, figures are relatively small for biodiversity, representing 3% of total private finance mobilised in 2022 (Figure 7.1) and 1% of total private finance mobilised on average over 2017-22 (as a reference, private finance mobilised for climate action represented 35% of total private finance mobilised, at USD 16.1 billion on average over the period). This may reflect the challenges associated with mobilising private sector financing specifically for biodiversity-related action, including public policy failures, lack of data for measuring impact and nature-related risk, issues with small-scale or non-commercial biodiversity investment opportunities, and the lack of a (readily available) pipeline of investment projects (World Bank Group, 2020[4]), as well as the lack of conducive enabling environments overall (see Box 3.2). Importantly, most biodiversity and natural resource challenges are location-specific, further creating difficulties in both identifying a problem and then replicating a solution, particularly for nature-based solutions. In addition, the lack of long-term funding and support further hampers the success and implementation of related projects (OECD, 2023[5]).

Despite these challenges, DAC members acknowledge the crucial role of mobilising private finance for biodiversity action and are working to understand the financing mechanisms involved and to overcome investment barriers to secure additional funding. For instance, Germany is supporting the Biodiversity Finance Accelerator Southern Africa in Malawi and Zambia, aiming to mobilise biodiversity investments by developing a pipeline of bankable market-based solutions, increasing the understanding of conservation finance and designing biodiversity financial leveraging instruments (IKI, 2024[6]). Further, it provides capacity building programmes and empowers biodiversity-friendly micro, small and medium-sized enterprises to access growth finance and amplify positive biodiversity impacts. Given the relevance of mobilising private finance for biodiversity, the OECD and DAC members will be explicitly focusing on this issue, looking closer into the issues mentioned in this chapter (OECD, forthcoming).

A growing number of DAC members mobilise private finance for biodiversity, increasing from just 3 DAC members in 2017 to 13[1] in 2022. However, the volume of mobilised funds remains concentrated among a few members. In 2022, three DAC members - namely the United States (74%), France (11%) and Australia (7%) - accounted for 93% of the total bilateral private finance mobilised for biodiversity-related activities. Similarly, only a few multilateral institutions stand out in this space, with most private finance mobilised for biodiversity-related action concentrated on a few providers.

Private finance for biodiversity was mostly mobilised in upper middle-income countries (62% of the total without considering unspecified allocations), followed by lower middle-income countries (25%) and least developed countries (13%), on average over 2017-22. In particular, Ecuador accounted for 50% of the total over the period, followed by Belize (18%), Cambodia (6%), the Democratic Republic of the Congo (4%) and Brazil (3%). Overall, the most targeted regions were Latin America and the Caribbean (73%), followed by Asia (13%) and Africa (12%).

Overall, in 2022, private finance was mobilised by a variety of leveraging mechanisms, yet mostly concentrated around guarantees (67%).[2] Other leveraging mechanisms applied include credit lines (9%), simple co-financing (8%), direct investment in companies and special purpose vehicles (9%), shares in structured or flat collective investment vehicles (5%, e.g. shares in the riskiest tranche, first loss share and other), and syndicated loans (less than 1%). See OECD (2020[7]) for more information on the methodologies for measuring the amounts mobilised from the private sector by ODF interventions, and Annex A for an overview of the leveraging mechanisms captured in OECD-DAC statistics.

Indeed, additional financial flows from a wide variety of sources are needed for sustainable development to meet biodiversity, oceans, degraded land and climate change targets, and enhance ecosystem services (G20 Rome Summit, 2021[8]). Creating favourable conditions to the development of financing mechanisms and private sector instruments (PSI) – as well as through partnerships, alliances and country-platforms – is also important to test, implement and capitalise upon and develop new initiatives that will allow private financing for biodiversity and natural resources to grow. Box 7.1 showcases some of the recent financial mechanisms used to mobilise private finance for biodiversity [e.g. debt-for-nature swaps], concerning the public and private sectors, and civil society, as well as efforts to strengthen PSI.

Box 7.1. Selected examples of mobilising private finance for biodiversity

Ecuador and the Galápagos Islands: Championing biodiversity financing

Ecuador is one of the most biodiverse countries in the world (WorldRainforests, 2023[9]; UNEP-WCMC, 2020[10]) and has recently accomplished the world's largest debt-for-nature conversion with support from the United States' Development Finance Corporation (DFC) and the Inter-American Development Bank (IDB), that will allow the country to reduce its debt burden and free up resources for long-term marine conservation in the Galápagos Islands, promote greater sustainability and improve livelihoods (IDB, 2024[11]).

The operation consists of an USD 85 million IDB guarantee and a USD 656 million DFC political-risk insurance to Ecuador to purchase existing public debt at better terms (IDB, 2024[11]). This debt purchase with cheaper financing will generate lifetime savings of more than USD 1.1 billion and savings to finance conservation activities for USD 323 million. These resources will be used to capitalise an endowment for the Galápagos Life Fund, which will finance conservation activities over the next 18.5 years in both the Galápagos Marine Reserve and the Reserva Marina Hermandad. Combined, the debt conversion and endowment will generate more than USD 450 million for marine conservation in the Galápagos Islands (DFC, 2023[12]). In addition, Credit Suisse Group provided structuring and technical advice for the transaction, Oceans Finance Company served as project manager and Pew Bertarelli Ocean Legacy as co-operating partner.

The growing momentum of debt-for-nature swaps

Debt-for-nature swaps (DNS) can be traced back to 1987 (World Bank, 1988[13]) but have a renewed momentum. A number of other countries – such as the Plurinational State of Bolivia, Costa Rica and the Philippines – have used DNS in the past to manage debt and improve their environmental protection and resilience in the process (World Bank, 1990[14]). Recently, such deals have created marine protected areas or funded other conservation measures in the waters of Belize, Barbados and the Seychelles (The Nature Conservancy, 2023[15]; The Nature Conservancy, 2023[16]; TNC, 2020[17]). Indeed, scaling up the number and size of DNS, along with complementary technical assistance, can help countries strengthen fiscal and environmental sustainability at a time when financing is scarce (IMF, 2023[18]; Jiang and Cao, 2024[19]).

Private sector instruments

At the DAC High Level Meeting in 2016, development ministers identified the private sector as a key partner to advance the international development agenda (OECD, 2016[20]). In pursuit of a more fitting enabling environment for innovative partnerships with private institutions, they agreed on a set of principles for reflecting donor effort in private sector instruments (PSI) in official development assistance (ODA). In 2023, after detailed negotiations, the DAC agreed on methods for counting donors' loans to the private sector, equity investments, guarantees and reimbursable grants in ODA on a grant-equivalent basis, as well as enhanced transparency provisions, ODA-integrity safeguards and monitoring provisions. This agreement is expected to incentivise donors' use of PSI for greater development impact.

Indeed, when deployed in support of nature-related solutions, PSI can help build biodiversity-friendly markets and mobilise additional finance. For example, the United Kingdom's vehicle Mobilising Finance for Forests extends PSI to combat deforestation and other environmentally unsustainable land-use practices in tropical forest regions that are contributing to global climate change and improved livelihoods (FMO, 2021[21]). In addition, the Netherlands' Dutch Fund for Climate and Development (DFCD) aims to promote climate-resilient growth through improving the well-being and prospects of vulnerable groups and the health of critical ecosystems such as river basins, tropical rainforests, marshlands and mangroves (DFCD, n.d.[22]). Recently, for example, DFCD has supported the development of integrated mangrove shrimp farms in Viet Nam, by assisting to de-risk the business, make it investment-ready and aligned with stakeholders' needs (DFCD, 2024[23]).

Private finance mobilisation for biodiversity can be achieved through varying financial structures and partnerships

There is no one-size-fits-all in the mobilisation of private finance for biodiversity. Indeed, private finance mobilisation for biodiversity can be achieved through different financial structures and mechanisms. For instance, facilities that promote public-private partnerships (PPPs) can mobilise private finance by creating joint ventures with government bodies, enterprises, non-governmental organisations and/or academia, together with development co-operation providers (Government of the Netherlands, 2023[24]). PPPs often help to de-risk financing for private financiers and can indicate strong government support of particular initiatives. For example, AGRI3 is a blended finance fund implemented by the partnership between the Dutch Ministry of Foreign Affairs (MINBUZA), the United Nations Environment Programme, the Dutch Entrepreneurial Development Bank (FMO), Rabobank and the Sustainable Trade Initiative which aims to unlock USD 1 billion towards sustainable agriculture, protecting forests and improving rural livelihoods by de-risking transactions (e.g. through guarantees and credit enhancement) and providing technical assistance (Agri3 Fund, n.d.[25]). In addition, MINBUZA is also supporting the Mobilising More for Climate programme, together with the International Union for Conservation of Nature, WWF and Topenbos International, seeking to connect entrepreneurs, companies, policy makers, investors, civil society organisations and local entrepreneurs to mobilise additional funding for nature-based solutions in developing countries, and to attract investments to implement these initiatives (MoMo4C, 2024[26]). Similarly, the United States Agency for International Development (USAID) together with the International Centre for Tropical Agriculture is supporting the Althelia Biodiversity Fund Brazil, a blended finance fund aiming to conserve biodiversity by de-risking allocations for investors (i.e. through guarantees and investing in junior tranches, respectively), and investments are managed by Mirova Natural Capital (Blended Finance Taskforce, 2019[27]).

Other structures include multi-donor funds and programmes. For instance, Aceli Africa is a financing facility promoting sustainable environment practices that offers de-risking financial incentives, defrays the transaction costs of lending and provides technical assistance to agri-SMEs, supported by grants from MINBUZA; the IKEA Foundation; the Swiss Agency for Development and Co-operation, the UK Foreign, Commonwealth and Development Office; and USAID (Aceli Africa, 2020[28]). Alternatively, other structures to mobilise private finance can involve multilateral biodiversity funds [e.g. the Global Environment Facility (GEF) and the KMGBF Fund, and the Green Climate Fund] or MDBs. For instance, the International Finance Corporation (as structurer and investor) and Banco Bilbao Vizcaya Argentaria (issuing bank) have partnered to issue a biodiversity bond and the resources will be used to finance projects focusing on reforestation, mangrove conservation, climate-smart agriculture and wildlife habitat restoration in Colombia (BBVA, 2024[29]). In addition, the World Bank has issued a Wildlife Conservation Bond consisting of an outcome-based bond that channels private capital to finance the conservation of endangered species, and together with GEF (which provides finance for the conservation success payment and de-risking) created an opportunity to attract private investment (WBG, 2024[30]). In particular, this so-called "Rhino Bond" focuses on achieving conservation outcomes by measuring an increase in black rhino populations in two protected areas in South Africa. The rhino growth rate will be calculated and verified by independent parties, Conservation Alpha and the Zoological Society of London respectively, over the bond term. The financial structure was developed with Credit Suisse Group, building on earlier preparatory work at the parks (World Bank, 2022[31]).

Finally, there are also multi-stakeholder partnerships spanning across a combination of public bilateral and multilateral donors and private funds, such as the example of Japan International Cooperation Agency's loan agreement with Ghana to promote an environmentally sustainable cocoa industry, along with co-financing by development finance and private finance institutions, namely the African Development Bank, the Development Bank of South Africa and the Italian National Promotion Bank "Cassa Depositi e Prestiti" (JICA, 2020[32]). In another example, the Nature Facility is a multi-partner trust fund between the United Nations Capital Development Fund; the United Nations Development Programme; and the United Nations Education, Science and Culture Organization, together with Cartier for Nature as its first donor, aiming to pool and channel resources to address the drivers of environmental degradation and ecological instability, with a focus on Natural World Heritage Sites and the ecosystems and people that interact with them (UNDP, 2024[33]). The Nature Facility benefits from lessons learnt from similar initiatives such as the Global Fund for Coral Reefs (GFCR, 2024[34]), and is supporting the blended finance project in Burundi's Kibira National Park by providing funding to the Kibira Foundation (a dedicated foundation to assist the park, co-managed by the government with participation of forest communities) to strengthen conservation and the sustainable exploitation of the forest's resources (UN, 2023[35]). The project also seeks to generate financial returns ("hydro-credits") from a hydropower public-private partnership that can be strategically re-invested into the Kibira Foundation, ensuring support for sustainable park management, peacebuilding and social cohesion activities.

References

Aceli Africa (2020), *Mobilizing capital, unlocking impact: Aceli Africa is building the finance market for an inclusive agricultural sector in Africa*, https://aceliafrica.org/. [28]

Agri3 Fund (n.d.), *Agri3 Fund*, https://agri3.com/about/ (accessed on 25 January 2023). [25]

BBVA (2024), *BBVA Colombia and IFC announce the financial sector's first biodiversity bond issue*, https://www.bbva.com/en/sustainability/bbva-colombia-and-ifc-announce-the-financial-sectors-first-biodiversity-bond-issue/ (accessed on 10 July 2024). [29]

Blended Finance Taskforce (2019), *Althelia Biodiversity Fund Brazil*, https://www.blendedfinance.earth/blended-finance-funds/2020/11/16/amazon-biodiviersity-fund (accessed on 10 July 2024). [27]

CBD (2022), *Kunming-Montreal Global Biodiversity Framework*, https://www.cbd.int/doc/c/e6d3/cd1d/daf663719a03902a9b116c34/cop-15-l-25-en.pdf (accessed on 15 July 2024). [1]

Corporation, U. (ed.) (2023), *Financial Close Reached in Largest Debt Conversion for Marine Conservation to Protect the Galápagos*, https://www.dfc.gov/media/press-releases/financial-close-reached-largest-debt-conversion-marine-conservation-protect (accessed on 3 July 2024). [12]

DFCD (2024), *Sowing prosperity in the Mekong Delta*, https://www.thedfcd.com/news/sowing-prosperity-in-the-mekong-delta/ (accessed on 14 July 2024). [23]

DFCD (n.d.), *Who we are: The DFCD*, https://www.thedfcd.com/ (accessed on 10 July 2024). [22]

FMO (2021), *About Mobilising Finance for Forests*, https://www.fmo.nl/about-mff (accessed on 4 July 2024). [21]

GFCR (2024), *Global Fund for Coral Reefs*, https://globalfundcoralreefs.org/ (accessed on 10 July 2024). [34]

Government of the Netherlands (2023), *Mobilised private (climate and biodiversity) finance*, https://www.government.nl/documents/reports/2023/06/30/mobilised-private-climate-and-biodiversity-finance (accessed on 10 July 2024). [24]

IDB (2024), *Ecuador Completes World's Largest Debt-for-Nature Conversion with IDB and DFC Support*, https://www.iadb.org/en/news/ecuador-completes-worlds-largest-debt-nature-conversion-idb-and-dfc-support (accessed on 9 May 2024). [11]

IKI (2024), *Biodiversity Finance Accelerator Southern Africa (BioFA)*, https://www.international-climate-initiative.com/en/project/biodiversity-finance-accelerator-southern-africa-biofa-img2020-iv-009-afri-biodiversity-finance-accelerator/ (accessed on 25 July 2024). [6]

IMF (2023), *Online Annex 5. Debt-for-Nature Swaps in Latin America and the Caribbean. Regional Economic Outlook*, https://www.imf.org/-/media/Files/Publications/REO/WHD/2023/October/English/onlineannex-5-en.ashx. (accessed on 1 July 2024). [18]

Jiang, X. and H. Cao (2024), "Implementing the debt-for-nature swaps for marine protected areas: case studies from Seychelles and Belize", *Humanities and Social Sciences Communications*, Vol. 11/1, https://doi.org/10.1057/s41599-024-02855-3. [19]

JICA (2020), *Signing of Loan Agreement for "Cocoa Value Chain Enhancement Project" in Ghana: Contributing to Enhancement of the Agricultural Value Chain and Related Industries*, https://www.jica.go.jp/Resource/english/news/press/2019/20200221_10_en.html (accessed on 10 July 2024). [32]

Meeting, G. (ed.) (2021), *G20 Environment Communiqué*, http://www.g20italy.org/wp-content/uploads/2021/07/2021_07_22_ITG20_ENV_Final.pdf (accessed on 3 July 2024). [8]

MoMo4C (2024), *Mobilising More for Climate*, https://www.momo4climate.org/ (accessed on 10 July 2024). [26]

OECD (2024), *OECD DAC Creditor Reporting System Statistics*, OECD.Stat, https://data-explorer.oecd.org/s/c. [3]

OECD (2024), "OECD Data Explorer", *Mobilised private finance for development*, https://data-explorer.oecd.org/vis?fs[0]=Topic%2C1%7CDevelopment%23DEV%23%7COfficial%20Development%20Assistance%20%28ODA%29%23DEV_ODA%23&pg=0&fc=Topic&bp=true&snb=13&df[ds]=dsDisseminateFinalDMZ&df[id]=DSD_MOB%40DF_MOBILISATION&df[ag]=OECD.DCD.FSD&df[vs]=. [2]

OECD (2023), *Scaling Up the Mobilisation of Private Finance for Climate Action in Developing Countries: Challenges and Opportunities for International Providers*, Green Finance and Investment, OECD Publishing, Paris, https://doi.org/10.1787/17a88681-en. [5]

OECD (2020), *DAC methodologies for measuring the amounts mobilised from the private sector by official development finance interventions*. [7]

OECD (2016), *DAC High Level Meeting Communiqué*, https://web-archive.oecd.org/2016-02-19/388307-DAC-HLM-Communique-2016.pdf (accessed on 4 July 2024). [20]

The Nature Conservancy (2023), *Case Study: Barbados Blue Bonds for Ocean Conservation*, https://www.nature.org/content/dam/tnc/nature/en/documents/TNC-Barbados-Debt-Conversion-Case-Study.pdf (accessed on 1 July 2024). [15]

The Nature Conservancy (2023), *Case Study: Belize Blue Bonds for Ocean Conservation*, https://www.nature.org/content/dam/tnc/nature/en/documents/TNC-Belize-Debt-Conversion-Case-Study.pdf (accessed on 1 July 2024). [16]

TNC (2020), *Seychelles Achieves 30 Percent Marine Conservation Commitment: New Protections Come From World's First Debt Refinancing for Ocean Conservation*, https://www.nature.org/en-us/about-us/where-we-work/africa/stories-in-africa/seychelles-conservation-commitment-comes-to-life/. [17]

UN (2023), *Investing in innovative approaches to advance peacebuilding in Burundi's Kibira National Park*, https://www.un.org/peacebuilding/content/investing-innovative-approaches-advance-peacebuilding-burundi%E2%80%99s-kibira-national-park (accessed on 10 July 2024). [35]

UNDP (2024), *NATURE FACILITY: Leveraging blended finance for nature*, https://www.undp.org/nature/our-flagship-initiatives/nature-facility (accessed on 10 July 2024). [33]

UNEP-WCMC (2020), *Megadiverse Countries*, https://www.biodiversitya-z.org/content/megadiverse-countries (accessed on 10 June 2024). [10]

WBG (2024), *Wildlife Conservation Bond*, https://treasury.worldbank.org/en/about/unit/treasury/ibrd/wildlife-conservation-bond (accessed on 10 July 2024). [30]

World Bank (2022), *Wildlife Conservation Bond mobilizes private capital to protect critically endangered rhinos*, https://thedocs.worldbank.org/en/doc/7039bd837e60e484fb3a93ea63951306-0340022022/original/CaseStudy-WildlifeConservationBond.pdf (accessed on 10 July 2024). [31]

World Bank (1990), *Debt-for-Nature Swaps*, Michael Ochiolin, https://documents1.worldbank.org/curated/en/300181468739253960/pdf/multi0page.pdf (accessed on 15 July 2024). [14]

World Bank (1988), *Debt for Nature Swaps: Overview and Discussion of Key Issues*, Stein Hansen, https://documents1.worldbank.org/curated/en/823691493257754828/pdf/Debt-for-nature-swaps-overview-and-discussion-of-key-issues.pdf (accessed on 25 July 2024). [13]

World Bank Group (2020), *Mobilizing private finance for nature*, https://thedocs.worldbank.org/en/doc/916781601304630850-0120022020/original/FinanceforNature28Sepwebversion.pdf (accessed on 2 April 2023). [4]

WorldRainforests (2023), *Countries with the highest biodiversity*, https://worldrainforests.com/03highest_biodiversity.htm (accessed on 26 December 2023). [9]

Notes

[1] The following DAC members have mobilised private finance for biodiversity over 2017-22: Australia, Austria, Belgium, Canada, Czech Republic, Finland, France, Germany, Korea, Portugal, Spain, Sweden, Switzerland, UK, US.

[2] Guarantees refer to legally binding agreements under which the guarantor agrees to pay part or the entire amount due on a loan, equity or other instrument in the event of non-payment by the obligor or loss of value in case of investment. The term guarantee refers to both guarantee and insurance scheme.

Annex A. Data coverage and sources

Official development assistance, other official flows and official development finance

The OECD Development Assistance Committee (DAC) Secretariat collects individual aid activities on official development assistance (ODA) and other official flows (OOF) in the *Creditor Reporting System* (CRS). ODA is defined as flows to countries on the DAC List of ODA Recipients and core contributions to multilateral development institutions provided by official or executive agencies on the List of ODA-eligible international organisations (OECD, 2021[1]). ODA must have the economic development and welfare of developing countries as its main objective and be concessional in character - either flowing as grants or concessional loans (i.e. softer than market terms). In turn, OOF comprises transactions from governments to developing countries that do not qualify as ODA, e.g. non-concessional sovereign loans (OECD, 2021[1]). This definition of OOF excludes official direct export credits. Together, the sum of bilateral ODA flows, bilateral OOF (except OOF grants and loans for commercial purposes), and all finance (grants and loans) by multilateral development institutions, define official development finance (ODF). As such, ODF is a broader measure of developing countries' official receipts for development purposes (OECD, 2021[1]).

Countries and institutions reporting to the OECD on their ODF flows include biodiversity-related information through the biodiversity Rio marker, as well as through two Sustainable Development Goal (SDG) tags (for marine and terrestrial biodiversity), and two biodiversity-related purpose codes (see below). In other cases, biodiversity-related information needs to be searched and verified manually in the CRS (e.g. through data mining).

Data sources: The biodiversity Rio marker, SDGs 14 and 15, biodiversity purpose codes, and keywords

The Rio marker on biodiversity

To date, the Rio markers represent the most comprehensive, publicly available activity-level data on biodiversity-related development finance from bilateral donors. Since 1998, the DAC monitors development finance targeting the objectives of the Rio Conventions, including the United Nations Convention on Biological Diversity (CBD), through four "Rio markers" [biodiversity, desertification, climate change mitigation and adaptation (the latter introduced in 2009); for more information on the markers, see OECD (2016[2]). The Rio markers were designed to track the degree to which members integrate environmental considerations into their development co-operation activities, and to support members in preparing their national reports to the Conventions. Reporting on the Rio markers is mandatory for ODA from DAC members (but not for OOF or for multilateral and bilateral providers beyond the DAC members reporting to the OECD). Coverage of OOF with the Rio markers for bilateral providers is limited (Casado-Asensio, Blaquier and Gualberti, 2024[3]).

For DAC members and countries and institutions voluntarily using the Rio markers, biodiversity-related activities ought to be screened and marked as either (i) targeting the objectives of the CBD, with a "principal objective" or a "significant objective"; or (ii) not targeting the objective (the activity has no relation with the marker). Activities marked as "principal" would not have been funded but for that objective; activities marked as "significant" have other primary objectives but have been formulated or adjusted to help meet biodiversity concerns.

The activities identified with the marker should promote at least one of the three objectives of the CBD, namely: 1) the conservation of biodiversity; 2) the sustainable use of its components (ecosystems, species or genetic resources); and 3) fair and equitable sharing of the benefits of the utilisation of genetic resources. The Rio marker methodology includes biodiversity-related finance from all sectors, not just the environmental sector. As such, an activity can be marked with the biodiversity Marker if it contributes to any of the following:

a) protecting or enhancing ecosystems, species or genetic resources through *in-situ* or *ex-situ* conservation, or remedying existing environmental damage;

b) integrating biodiversity and ecosystem services concerns within recipient countries' development objectives and economic decision making, through institution building, capacity development, strengthening the regulatory and policy framework, or research;

c) developing countries' efforts to meet their obligations under the Convention (OECD, 2019[4]).

As mentioned above, an activity scores "principal" if it directly and explicitly aims to achieve one or more of the above three criteria. Alternatively, the marker identifies projects that can have "significant" co-benefits for biodiversity but for which biodiversity is not the primary focus (e.g. a project focused on enhancing agricultural production, while training smallholder farmers to combine native vegetation with crops for higher outputs and biodiversity protection). For a project to be identified as "significant" it must also comply with the eligibility criteria for the biodiversity marker, even if it is not the project's primary focus.

It should be noted that much of the project-level ODF delivered with the biodiversity marker can contribute to one or more of the other Rio markers (e.g. aid to biodiversity often creates positive impacts for desertification and/or for climate change mitigation and adaptation) and/or other areas (e.g. governance, gender, disaster risk reduction). Thus, the presentation of more than one marker allows for the possibility of overlaps across them. For the purpose of doing deep-dive analyses into cross-cutting issues, the other markers used in this report are the climate change Rio markers [i.e. climate change adaptation and climate change mitigation (OECD, n.d.[5])] and the gender equality policy marker [i.e. aid activities targeting gender equality and women's empowerment (OECD, 2016[6])].

The Rio markers were designed to track the degree to which members are integrating and mainstreaming environmental considerations into their development co-operation activities, and thus apply to the entirety of an activity reported – not to the allocation of finance associated with the biodiversity-specific component of that activity. Alternatively, in reporting against quantified international finance goals [such as the CBD's Aichi Target 20 on development finance and Target 19a of the Kunming-Montreal Global Biodiversity Framework (KMGBF)], many DAC members report only a proportion of their ODF targeting biodiversity as a "significant" objective, estimating this through applying coefficients to adjust the share of finance reported (Casado-Asensio, Blaquier and Gualberti, 2024[3]). A coefficient is applied because the Rio marker data applies to the entire activity reported by the provider, not the finance associated with the biodiversity-specific component of that activity. There is no agreed definition or common approach for this practice, but the most common coefficient applied is 40% to countries' "significant" flows (Casado-Asensio, Blaquier and Gualberti, 2024[3]), which will be used to present progress against the contribution of development finance to KMGBF Target 19a, along with the full account of "principal" flows.

Reporting on biodiversity-related SDGs

A specific field for reporting on the SDGs exists in the CRS [for more information see OECD (2020[7])]. This includes data on SDG 14 "Life below water" and SDG 15 "Life on land", including their targets. SDG 14 aims to "conserve and sustainably use the oceans, seas and marine resources" by, for example, reducing marine pollution, sustainably managing and protecting marine and coastal ecosystems, and ending overfishing. SDG 15 aims to "sustainably manage forests, combat desertification, halt and reverse land degradation, halt biodiversity loss" by, for example, reducing the degradation of natural habitats, preventing the loss of biodiversity, supporting efforts to combat poaching and trafficking of protected species, and scaling up financial resources to conserve and sustainably use biodiversity and ecosystems. Reporting on the SDG focus in the CRS[1] is recent (introduced in 2018), experimental and voluntary (and can be done at the goal or target level) (OECD, 2021[1]); the heterogeneity in reporting quality of this field implies that data extracted from this field may be inconsistent across donors.

Moreover, reporting on SDG focus areas often includes SDGs 14 and 15 along with many other SDGs, thus limiting the precision of estimates derived from this field. Notwithstanding, they still help fill missing data gaps and provide additional information (e.g. to identify non-biodiversity-marked projects and for countries and institutions that do not use the marker). For the purpose of this analysis, fields with either SDG 14 or 15 were verified manually and retained, and when considered as "significant-like", a coefficient was applied when counting these numbers. For the analysis on climate change, moreover, information reported on the SDG 13 was also included in this analysis; as was SDG 5 used for the analysis on gender equality.

To ensure the data added are robust, a manual revision of the data reported against the SDGs ensured consistency with reported elements and the definition of the Rio marker on biodiversity (i.e. the objective or description of the activity relates to the objectives of the CBD) and following the guidance described in OECD (2019[4]). Following this logic, estimates mainly considered allocable flows (notably those targeting the ODA-eligible co-operation modalities, i.e. A02, B01, B03, B04, C01, D01, D02, E01).

Biodiversity-related purpose codes

The CRS has a taxonomy of purpose codes which identifies the sector that the activity intends to support (OECD, n.d.[8]). In the case of biodiversity, the CRS has two purpose codes that target biodiversity under 410 (general environmental protection), namely 41020 (biosphere protection, which includes air pollution control, ozone layer preservation, marine pollution control); and 41030 (biodiversity, includes natural reserves and actions in the surrounding areas, other measures to protect endangered or protected species and their habitats, e.g. wetland preservation). For multilateral institutions, flows available under the biodiversity purpose code were assimilated to "principal-like" activities (and flows were counted in their entirety) while those under the biosphere purpose codes depended on a case-by-case approach.

Keyword searches

Beyond the use of the biodiversity Rio marker, purpose codes and SDGs, biodiversity-related information was also searched manually in the CRS by applying a keyword search on merged descriptive data fields, such as project titles and descriptions (in English, French and Spanish). This was primarily used for multilateral institutions, which helps make use of the full informative content in the database and increase the likelihood that all projects relevant for biodiversity are captured, while maintaining the integrity of the CRS database and information contained therein (see Table A A.1.).

There are inherent limitations when using keyword searches on text descriptions of the CRS. Due to missing words, incomplete or erroneous reporting, and lack of consistency in the project description, the procedure cannot guarantee that all biodiversity-related projects are detected. The selection of keywords aims at accuracy, as well as granularity. In the case of multilateral institutions, keywords were separated into two categories: a first category of keywords related closely with "principal-like" biodiversity-related activities (e.g. activities related to conservation, protection and restoration of biodiversity, or illegal wildlife trade). A second category of keywords aimed at capturing "significant-like" biodiversity-related activities;

that is, activities where biodiversity aspects are mainstreamed into other sectors (and a coefficient was applied when counting these numbers). The aim of applying this two-category keyword approach was to maximise data disaggregation while balancing the risk of capturing projects that are not beneficial or related to biodiversity, with the risk of discarding actual biodiversity-related projects. To ensure the robustness of this methodology, moreover, activities identified through the keyword search were individually assessed to verify their fit with the definition of the Rio marker on biodiversity and also referred to the marker indicative tables. When an activity did not fit with this definition, or when information was missing or partial, it was excluded from the analysis.

Table A A.1. Biodiversity-related keywords applied to identify biodiversity-related activities

Classification	Biodiversity-related keywords
English "principal-like"	30BY30, Amazon conservation, antelope conservation, anti-poaching, biodiversity, bio-diversity, biosphere, Bird Conservation, Cartagena protocol, CBD, CCAMLR, oceans conservation, CITES, coastal protected areas, coastal protection, coastal wetlands protection, combat IUU, combating fish crimes, combating wildlife, combatting IUU, combatting wildlife, Community conservation, Community Marine Park, Community-based conservation, conflict management of elephants, conservation and Sustainable Use of the Threatened Savanna Woodland, conservation area, conservation forests, conservation landscape, conservation of animal genetic resources, Conservation of Antarctic Marine Living Resources, conservation of aquatic ecosystems, Conservation of Endemic Flora, conservation of habitats and species, Conservation of Land Resources, conservation of mangroves, Conservation of Nature, conservation of orangutans, conservation of the Asiatic Cheetah, conservation of wildcats, conservation project, conservation-commerce model , conserve orangutans, Convention on Biological Diversity, Convention on Biological Diversity, coral bleaching, coral reef protection, coral reef rehabilitation, coral reef rescue, critically endangered, destructive fishing, ecological connectivity, ecological conservation, ecological protection, ecological restoration, ecosystem conservation, Ecosystem Landscape Approach, ecosystem rehabilitation, ecosystems protection, elephant conservation, elimination of mercury, endangered flora, Endangered Species, endemic land-birds, Endangered species, fauna corridor, forest and landscape restoration, forest conservation, forest ecosystem, forest friendly livelihood, forest landscape restoration, forest restoration, genetic resources strengthening, gibbon conservation, goal 14, goal 15, grassland conservation, habitat corridor, habitat protection, habitat restoration, hornbill conservation, human wildlife, human-animal, human-elephant coexistence, human-elephant conflict, human-wildlife, illegal deforestation, illegal fish, illegal fishing, illegal hunting, illegal trafficking of wildlife, illegal wildlife, IUCN, IUU fishing, IWT, jaguar, Kimberley Process Certification Scheme, lake conservation, Land Degradation Neutrality, landscape conservation, landscape restoration, leopard, mangrove, Marine Conservation, Marine park, Minamata Convention, MPA , Nagoya Protocol, national park, native forest, natural forest, natural habitat, natural heritage, natural resource conservation, nature conservation, nature conservation, nature protection, nature reserve, NBSAPs, payment for environmental services, payments for ecosystem services, peatland restoration, pet trade, plant conservation, poaching, pollinator, preservation of the environment, preventing forest loss, protected area, protection of its natural resources, Ramsar, recovery of natural capital, reef restoration, resource conservation, restoration of coral, restoring forest, rhino, sdg 14, sdg 15, sdg14, sdg15, sea turtle, Secure Wetland Ecosystems, Shorebird Conservation, soil conservation, Solutions based on nature, species conservation, Strengthening natural reserve, sustainably manage natural resources and ecosystems, The Nature Conservancy (TNC), tiger, trafficking of wildlife, unreported and unregulated fishing, Watershed Conservation, watershed rehabilitation, wetland protected, wetland protection, wetland resilience, Wetlands International, wilderness, wildlife, WWF
English "significant-like"	adequate management of irrigation water, agri-environmental, agrobiology, agroecology, anti-poaching, bioeconomy, blue action fund, blue spaces, bushmeat, Caribbean Biodiversity Fund, conservation agriculture, conservation and use of plant, CZM, decreasing erosion, deforestation, degradation of forests, degraded ecosystems, degraded forest, degraded landscape, dryland sustainable, Earth Observation, EbA, ecological footprint, ecological integrity, ecosystem approach, ecosystem functions and services, ecosystem services, ecosystem values, ecosystem-based, Ecotourism, ecotourism, EMEC, enhancement of natural, environment improvement, environment protection, environment rehabilitation, environmental conservation, environmental crime, environmental degradation, environmental pollution, environmental protection, environmentally sensitive areas, environmentally sustainable, farmland sustainable utilisation, fisheries intelligence, forest fragmentation, forest resource development, fragile lands, freshwater ecosystems, GEF, global biodiversity framework, Global Environment Facility, green space, green wall, healthy forest, hunting practices, hunting the hunters, illegal charcoal, illegal crop, integrated coastal management, integrated coastal zone management, integrated ecosystem, integrated forest, integrated land water, integrated river basin management, land and ecosystem management, land degradation, land protect, land restoration, land use and restoration, management of forests, management of landscapes, management of peat-swamp, marine ecosystem, marine environment, mercury, natural resource management, nature based tourism, nature-based solutions, nature-based tourism, organic agriculture, organic cereal, organic certification, organic coffee, organic farm, organic farming, ozone depletion, REDD, reducing vulnerability of natural resource, reduction of soil erosion, reforestation, resilience of fisheries, resilience of wetlands, resilient agroforestry, resilient fisheries, resilient landscape, responsible fishing, seas

Classification	Biodiversity-related keywords
	sustainable management, SLM, smart agriculture, sustainability of mangrove, sustainable agriculture, sustainable and socially acceptable fish, sustainable aqua, sustainable bio-energy, sustainable biomass, sustainable coastal, sustainable cropland, sustainable development of natural resources, sustainable dryland, sustainable environment, sustainable fish, sustainable forest, sustainable fuelwood management, sustainable game management, sustainable harvest, sustainable land, sustainable landscape, sustainable livestock, sustainable management of bycatch, sustainable management of fisheries, sustainable management of lakes, sustainable management of natural resources, sustainable management of peatland, sustainable management of tuna, sustainable management of wildlife, sustainable mangrove management, sustainable marine, sustainable natural, sustainable supply chains for marine commodities, sustainable timber, sustainable use of medicinal plants, sustainable use of natural resource, sustainable use of peatland, sustainable use of PGRFA, sustainable utilisation of plant genetic resources, sustainable watershed, sustainable wildlife management, sustainably managing the natural, United Nations Development Programme's Biodiversity Finance, vulnerable ecosystems, water conservation, water resources conservation, watershed conservation, watershed management, wetland ecosystem, wildfire management,
Spanish "principal-like"	área protegida, áreas protegida, biodiversidad, conectividad ecológica, conservación de anfibios, conservación de la biodiversidad, conservación forestal, conservar la biodiversidad, Convenio sobre la Diversidad Biológica, corredores biologicos, ecoturismo, en peligro de extinción, humedales protegidos, murciélago, patrimonio natural, pesca ilegal, protección del medio ambiente, vida silvestre
Spanish "significant-like"	Agricultura de conservación, agricultura orgánica, agroambiental, agroecología, agrosilvicultura resiliente, animales confiscados, bioandes, bioeconomía, bosque degradado, bosque integrado, bosque saludable, bosque sostenible, café orgánico, capital natural, carbono azul, carne de animales silvestres, cereal orgánico, certificación orgánica, conservación de cuencas hidrográficas, conservación de recursos, conservación del agua, Convención de las Naciones Unidas para Combatir la Desertificación, cosecha sostenible, deforestación, degradación ambiental, degradación de la tierra, degradación de los bosques, delitos ambientales, desarrollo de ecosistemas integrados de montañas, diversidad biológica, diversidad genética, economía azul, ecosistema de humedales, ecosistema marino, ecosistemas de agua dulce, ecosistemas de bosques de montaña, ecosistemas degradados, ecosistemas vulnerables, enfoque basado en ecosistemas, enfoque ecosistémico, evaluaciones de impacto ambiental, fondo de acción azul, fondo de biodiversidad del caribe, Fondo para el Medio Ambiente Mundial, funciones y servicios ecosistémicos, gestión ambiental sostenible, gestión integral de tierras, gestión sostenible de la tierra, gestión sostenible de la vida silvestre, gestión sostenible de las turberas, horticultura sostenible, huella ecológica, intercambio de información y datos oceanográficos, inundaciones costeras, madera sostenible, manejo costero integrado, manejo de incendios forestales, medio ambiente sostenible, mejorar la tierra, natural sostenible, no maderable, pago por servicios de cuencas, paisaje sostenible, pérdida de biodiversidad, pérdida de hábitat, plantas medicinales, prácticas de gestión de recursos naturales, reducción del riesgo de desastres, restauración de hábitat cosecha, servicios ecosistémicos, silvicultura sostenible, silvicultura y conservación, solución basada en la naturaleza, tierra sostenible, tierra y conservación del agua, tierras frágiles tigre, uso y restauración de la tierra
French "principal-like"	aires marines, aires marines protégées, aire protégé, aires protégées, Biodiversité, conservation des écosystèmes, conservation des écosystèmes forestiers, conservation de la biodiversité, conservation de la forêt primaire, conservation des espèces migratrices, conservation des petits cétacés, conservation des sols, conservation des éléphants, conservation des terres, conservation du paysage, contre le braconnage, exploitation illégale des ressources naturelles, faune sauvage, Parc National, Parcs nationaux, perte de la nature, préservation forêt, protection de l'environnement, réhabilitation du parc national, réhabilitation parc, UICN, Union International pour la Conservation de la Nature, utilisation durable du parc national, zones protégées
French "significant-like"	adaptation basée sur les écosystèmes (AbE), agriculture durable, agroécologiques, aménagement durable du territoire, secteur de l'environnement, crédit de nature, crédit environnement, crédit verte, gestion durables des terres, gestion intégrée des forêts, muraille verte, pastorales durables, performance environnementale, ressources naturelles, restauration écologique, sols dégradés, utilisation durable des forêts

Notes: The keywords enumerated were ran within strings of a same formula. As such, some keywords within the list might not have captured activities. Most multilateral institutions report to the OECD CRS dataset in English or Spanish. This analysis found some relevant activities reported in French, and thus included French keywords when potentially suitable.

Source: The list of keywords was derived from a literature review and through the review of common words used in the CRS database of biodiversity-marked projects.

Other remarks on the data sources used

Reporting on the biodiversity Rio marker is mandatory for DAC members, further agreeing that any activity reported with the biodiversity purpose code (41030) must also be reported with the biodiversity Rio marker for coherence. Data from 2015-20 reflect an accurate use of both markers, with less than 1% inconsistency starting from 2020 – although further efforts are needed to address inconsistencies in how countries apply and interpret the Rio markers and the SDGs. Indeed, it is important to note that these estimates only provide an approximation of total "principal" and "significant" objective shares – as a portion of biodiversity-related ODA is reported against the SDGs and not the Rio markers over 2018-21. This, in turn, means that DAC members reporting on the SDGs could explore whether projects targeting SDGs 14 and 15 could also be reported against the biodiversity Rio marker, and then assigned a "principal" or "significant" score.

However, this is not the case for multilateral institutions. For multilateral institutions, the use of the biodiversity Rio marker is voluntary, resulting in inconsistent and incomparable reporting. As such, activities marked with the biodiversity purpose code are not necessarily marked with the biodiversity Rio marker, resulting in 17% and 39% (in 2015 and 2021, respectively) of activities marked with the biodiversity purpose code not being marked with the biodiversity Rio marker.

Finally, some of these data sources are insufficient to track elements of relevance for biodiversity (e.g. marine and terrestrial biodiversity) or promote further disaggregation (e.g. exploring whether certain sector codes, such as forestry or general environmental protection, could be revised to improve granularity).

Time range of analysis

This report provides a quantitative analysis of recent trends of biodiversity-related development finance (2015-22). The analysis could be provided on a disbursement or commitment basis. A commitment is a firm written obligation by a government or official agency, backed by the appropriation or availability of the necessary funds to provide resources of a specified amount under specified financial terms and conditions, and for specified purposes for the benefit of a recipient country or multilateral agency. The estimates presented in this report are based on a commitment basis both for bilateral DAC members and multilateral institution providers and over the period 2015-22.

There are additional caveats regarding the time range applied in this analysis:

- OOF data reported to the CRS is still limited to a few donors, compared to ODA data.
- CRS data for SDGs 14 and 15 were only introduced in 2019 for 2018 activities (OECD, 2018[9]), hence data will only be available for the 2018-22 period.
- On the mobilisation of private finance by ODF, data are available from 2012, although quality and coverage improved significantly after 2017 (e.g. sector, marker and other descriptive fields) when related data collections were integrated into regular CRS reporting. In addition, reporting for the biodiversity Rio marker is not mandatory for mobilisation data.
- For philanthropic foundations, data are collected and published at the level of individual grants and programme-related investments, and - for most private providers - screened annually by the OECD Secretariat using the Rio marker methodology and on the SDG focus. While the dataset used for this analysis includes statistics for 2015-22, coverage for the period 2015-16 is limited compared to 2017-22. In fact, prior to 2015, the Bill & Melinda Gates Foundation was the only foundation reporting financial flows to the CRS.

Countries and institutions reporting to the OECD on biodiversity

The analysis looks at available data on bilateral donors (DAC and non-DAC), multilateral providers, mobilisation data and private philanthropies that report to the OECD:

- The CRS includes data on 32 DAC members (OECD, 2024[10]) that are mandated to use the biodiversity marker on ODA reported: Australia, Austria, Belgium, Canada, Czechia, Denmark, EU institutions (excluding the European Investment Bank from 2021), Finland, France, Germany, Greece, Hungary, Iceland, Ireland, Italy, Japan, Korea, Luxembourg, the Netherlands, New Zealand, Norway, Poland, Portugal, the Slovak Republic, Slovenia, Spain, Sweden, Switzerland, the United Kingdom and the United States. In particular, in 2021, Estonia and Lithuania were not yet DAC members, given that they provided 2021 data before the reporting deadline while already being DAC members, their 2021 data are reflected as DAC members. Additionally, 30 DAC members also report to the *Total Official Support for Sustainable Development* (TOSSD) database.

- In addition, 21 other countries and territories also report to the OECD using the CRS, of which only 8 have used the biodiversity marker to date: Azerbaijan, Cyprus, Estonia (until 2020), Latvia, Liechtenstein, Lithuania (until 2020), Monaco, Romania, Qatar and the United Arab Emirates. Other countries captured as contributing to biodiversity-related activities include: Bulgaria, Croatia, Israel, Kazakhstan, Kuwait, Malta, Türkiye, Saudi Arabia and Thailand. In addition, 27 countries report to the TOSSD, of which 9 contributed to biodiversity-related activities over 2019-22: Brazil, Chile, Costa Rica, the Dominican Republic, Ecuador, Indonesia, Kazakhstan, Mexico and Peru.
- For OOF, to date, Austria, Belgium, Canada, Finland, France, Germany, Norway, Sweden, Switzerland, the United Kingdom and the United States have reported biodiversity-related activities. In addition, 26 countries have reported their activities with SDGs 14 and 15 to date.
- More than 60 multilateral institutions have been reporting to the OECD-DAC CRS, of which 42 are reflected as providing biodiversity-related contributions. In particular, 16 have used the biodiversity marker, namely: Adaptation Fund (AF), Arab Fund for Economic and Social Development (AFESD), Asian Forest Cooperation Organisation, Development Bank of Latin America (CAF), Food and Agriculture Organisation (FAO), Global Environment Facility (GEF), Green Climate Fund (GCF), Inter-American Development Bank (IDB), IDB Invest, International Bank for Reconstruction and Development (IBRD), International Development Association (IDA), International Fund for Agricultural Development (IFAD), Islamic Development Bank (IsDB), Nordic Development Fund (NDF), United Nations Development Programme (UNDP), and World Tourism Organisation (WTO). Other multilateral institutions retained as providing biodiversity-related data (biodiversity purpose codes, SDG 14 and/or 15, key words) include: African Development Bank (AfDB), African Development Fund (ADF), Arab Bank for Economic Development in Africa (BADEA), Asian Development Bank (AsDB), Asian Forest Cooperation Organisation, Asian Infrastructure Investment Bank (AIIB), Caribbean Development Bank (CDB), Central American Bank for Economic Integration (CABEI), Consultative Group on International Agricultural Research (CGIAR), Climate Investment Funds (CIFs), European Investment Bank (EIB), European Bank for Reconstruction and Development (EBRD), Global Green Growth Institute (GGGI), International Finance Corporation (IFC), International Labour Organisation (ILO), Joint Sustainable Development Goals Fund (JSDGF), OPEC Fund for International Development (OFID), UN Peacebuilding Fund (UPF), United Nations Environment Programme (UNEP), United Nations Industrial Development Organization (UNIDO), United Nations Children's Fund (UNICEF), United Nations Economic Commission for Europe (UNECE), United Nations Conference on Trade and Development (UNCTAD), World Food Programme (WFP), WTO - International Trade Centre (WTO-ITC). Additional contributions were captured from multilateral institutions reporting to the TOSSD database (paying attention to avoid double counting): CABEI, CAF, GGGI, IFAD and Interpol, out of 64 institutions reporting to this database.
- The CRS includes data on finance flows reported by 47 philanthropic foundations, of which 40 provided data on biodiversity-related flows (biodiversity purpose codes or biodiversity marker or SDG 14 or 15), namely: Arcadia Fund, Arcus Foundation, BBVA Microfinance Foundation, Bernard van Leer Foundation, Bezos Earth Fund, Bill and Melinda Gates Foundation, Bloomberg Family Foundation, Carnegie Corporation of New York, Charity Projects Ltd (Comic Relief), Children's Investment Fund Foundation, Citi Foundation, David and Lucile Packard Foundation, Fondation Botnar, Ford Foundation, Gatsby Charitable Foundation, Gordon and Betty Moore Foundation, German Postcode Lottery, Grameen Crédit Agricole Foundation, H&M Foundation, Howard G. Buffett Foundation, IKEA Foundation, John D. and Catherine T. MacArthur Foundation, La Caixa Banking Foundation, Laudes Foundation, Margaret A. Cargill Foundation, Mastercard Foundation, MAVA Foundation, McKnight Foundation, Norwegian Postcode Lottery, Michael and Susan Dell

Foundation, Oak Foundation, Omidyar Network Fund, Inc., Open Society Foundations, Postcode Lottery Group (Dutch Postcode Lottery), People's Postcode Lottery, Swedish Postcode Lottery, Rockefeller Foundation, UBS Optimus Foundation, Wellcome Trust and William and Flora Hewlett Foundation. For more information on private philanthropy for sustainable development see OECD (2023[11]).

Total Official Support for Sustainable Development (TOSSD) data

TOSSD is an international standard for measuring the full array of resources to promote sustainable development in developing countries. It is designed to monitor both cross-border resources (Pillar I) and regional and global expenditures in support of sustainable development (Pillar II). TOSSD includes both concessional and non-concessional support, from multilateral and bilateral providers, including DAC members, South-South and triangular co-operation providers (TOSSD, 2024[12]). Importantly, some providers submit data both to the CRS and TOSSD through a single data submission. From 2024 onwards, the TOSSD standard is maintained and improved by the International Forum on TOSSD (IFT), hosted by the OECD.

TOSSD was adopted in March 2022 as a data source for the SDG global indicator framework (i.e. SDG indicator 17.3.1) to measure sustainable development support for "Additional financial resources mobilised for developing countries from multiple sources", increasing the visibility and transparency of official resources and private finance mobilised by official interventions.

The first comprehensive set of TOSSD data, for 2019, was published in 2021. As TOSSD consists exclusively of finance that contributes to enhancing sustainability defined as contributing to one or more SDGs, the reporting standard includes mandatory reporting on areas of SDG focus for reported projects. This requirement implies that TOSSD data are useful in evaluating contributions towards SDGs 14 and 15. However, data remain available only for the most recent years of analysis. Furthermore, the practice of reporting on SDG focus areas also leads to large projects being reported to be relevant for SDG 14 along other SDGs. TOSSD data are, therefore, not equivalent in scope and applicability to the methodology presented earlier but can provide complementary information. This report provides data on Pillar I from providers beyond the DAC (e.g. South-South and triangular co-operation).

In 2024, the International Forum on TOSSD agreed on the inclusion of a keyword to better track biodiversity-related support. The keyword aims to "to identify activities that promote one or more objectives of the Convention on Biological Diversity of the United Nations: conservation of biodiversity, sustainable use of its components (ecosystems, species or genetic resources) and/or the fair and equitable sharing of the benefits of the utilisation of genetic resources including by appropriate transfer of relevant technologies, taking into account all rights over those resources and technologies, and by appropriate funding." [Paragraph 92 of the TOSSD reporting instructions (TOSSD, 2024[13])].

Private finance mobilised by DAC countries' official development finance interventions

In the OECD-DAC statistics, mobilisation reflects the principles of causality between private finance made available for a specific project and an official intervention (OECD, 2021[14]). Data on the amounts of finance mobilised by DAC countries' ODF interventions are collected through regular CRS data collection for syndicated loans, guarantees, shares in collective investment vehicles, direct investment in companies, credit lines, project finance and simple co-financing arrangements (for further details see Table A A.2.). The methodologies for reporting on amounts mobilised are instrument-specific (OECD, 2021[1]), and include a pro-rated attribution as to avoid double counting in cases where more than one official provider is involved in a project mobilising private finance. The amounts mobilised from the private sector cover all private finance mobilised by ODF interventions regardless of the origin of the private funds (provider country, recipient country, third country). Private finance mobilised for biodiversity is identified when the DAC member reporting used the biodiversity marker, biodiversity purpose codes and keywords found in project descriptions and specific channels (e.g. Biodiversity International, Conservation International, The Nature Conservancy).

Table A A.2. Role and use of leveraging mechanisms

Leveraging mechanism	Definition	Underlying financial instruments used by public finance providers	Typical mobilised private finance
Syndicated loans	Syndicated loans are defined as loans provided by a group of lenders (a syndicate) which works together to provide funds to a single borrower.	Standard loans, subordinated loans	Private lenders participating in the loan syndication.
Guarantees	Guarantees are legally binding agreements under which the guarantor agrees to pay part of or the entire amount due on a loan, equity or other instrument in the event of non-payment by the obligor or loss of value in case of investment.	Guarantees and other unfunded contingent liabilities	Private equity investments and loans to special purpose vehicles (SPVs) and companies as well as portfolios of private local finance institutions.
Shares in collective investment vehicles (CIVs)	Shares in CIVs represent investments in pooling vehicles, such as investment funds and facilities, which typically use such finance to foster local small and medium-sized enterprise (SME) development.	Equity investments, loans and mezzanine finance (rarely)	Private equity investments in CIVs.
Direct investments in companies and SPVs	In the context of project finance, these mechanisms refer to mobilising private investments in SPVs, which are neither covered by official guarantors nor part of a syndicated loan. Beyond project finance, direct investment in companies refers to loans, mezzanine finance and equity investments in enterprises alongside with private investors to provide liquidity for expansion purposes.	Equity investments, mezzanine finance, standard loans, bonds and other debt instruments	In the context of project finance: private equity investments or private debt financing in SPVs (if not through syndicated loans). Beyond project finance: private debt financing (not syndicated) and equities invested in enterprises.
Credit lines	Credit lines refer to a standing credit amount which can be drawn upon by borrowers (typically local finance institutions) for on-lending purposes, mainly to SMEs.	Standard loans, subordinated loans	Top-up funds by private local finance institutions and in certain cases also equity investments in the end borrowers (if required).
Simple co-financing arrangements	Simple co-financing arrangements refer to various business partnerships, business-to-business programmes, business surveys, matching programmes, co-financing of specific projects and similar arrangements where official providers extend finance in co-financing with the private sector.	Standard grants, standard loans	Private co-finance of specific projects in the field or in the context of business partnerships.

Source: OECD (2023[15]), *Scaling Up the Mobilisation of Private Finance for Climate Action in Developing Countries: Challenges and Opportunities for International Providers*, https://dx.doi.org/10.1787/17a88681-en.

Recipient country analyses

The DAC list of ODA recipients for 2015-22 can be found in the *DAC List of ODA Recipients* (OECD, n.d.[16]).

Small island developing states country coverage

A total of 35 small island developing states (SIDS) are included in this report. In 2022, 32 SIDS were categorised as eligible in the DAC List of ODA Recipients (OECD, 2024[17]). These are Belize, Cabo Verde, the Comoros, Cuba, Dominica, the Dominican Republic, Fiji, Grenada, Guinea-Bissau, Guyana, Haiti, Jamaica, Kiribati, the Maldives, the Marshall Islands, Mauritius, Micronesia, Montserrat, Nauru, Niue, Palau, Papua New Guinea, Saint Lucia, Saint Vincent and the Grenadines, Samoa, São Tomé and Príncipe, the Solomon Islands, Suriname, Timor-Leste, Tonga, Tuvalu, and Vanuatu. As the analysis covers the period 2015-22, some results include data from the Seychelles, the Cook Islands, and Antigua and Barbuda, which graduated from the list in 2018, 2020 and 2022, respectively.

References

Casado-Asensio, J., D. Blaquier and G. Gualberti (2024), "Stock Take Report on Members' Reporting Practices on Biodiversity-related Development Finance and Reporting against International Obligations", *DCD/DAC/ENV(2024)1/REV1/FINAL*, https://one.oecd.org/document/DCD/DAC/ENV(2024)1/REV1/FINAL/en/pdf. [3]

OECD (2024), *Development Assistance Committee (DAC)*, https://www.oecd.org/dac/development-assistance-committee/ (accessed on 19 June 2024). [10]

OECD (2024), *History of DAC Lists of aid recipient countries*, https://web-archive.oecd.org/temp/2024-02-12/75435-historyofdaclistsofaidrecipientcountries.htm (accessed on 10 July 2024). [17]

OECD (2023), *Private philanthropy for sustainable development, 2018-20: Data and analysis*, OECD Publishing, https://www.oecd.org/dac/private-philanthropy-sustainable-development.pdf. [11]

OECD (2023), *Scaling Up the Mobilisation of Private Finance for Climate Action in Developing Countries: Challenges and Opportunities for International Providers*, Green Finance and Investment, OECD Publishing, Paris, https://doi.org/10.1787/17a88681-en. [15]

OECD (2021), *Converged Statistical Reporting Directives for the Creditor Reporting System and the Annual DAC Questionnaire, DCD/DAC/STAT(2020)44/FINAL*, https://one.oecd.org/document/DCD/DAC/STAT(2020)44/FINAL/en/pdf (accessed on 1 July 2024). [1]

OECD (2021), *Development Co-operation Report 2021: Shaping a Just Digital Transformation*, OECD Publishing, Paris, https://doi.org/10.1787/ce08832f-en. [14]

OECD (2020), *Draft Handbook for reporting the SDG focus of development co-operation activities*, https://www.oecd.org/officialdocuments/publicdisplaydocumentpdf/?cote=DCD/DAC/STAT(20 (accessed on 15 June 2024). [7]

OECD (2019), *Indicative table for the Rio Marker for Biodiversity*, https://www.oecd.org/officialdocuments/publicdisplaydocumentpdf/?cote=DCD/DAC/STAT(2018)26/REV1&docLanguage=En (accessed on 1 September 2022). [4]

OECD (2018), *Revision of the reporting directives: selections relating ot the approved SDG focus field and changes to policy markers and types of aid*, https://one.oecd.org/document/DCD/DAC/STAT(2018)52/en/pdf. [9]

OECD (2016), *Handbook on the OECD-DAC Gender Equality Policy Marker*, https://www.oecd.org/dac/gender-development/Handbook-OECD-DAC-Gender-Equality-Policy-Marker.pdf (accessed on 15 July 2024). [6]

OECD (2016), *Questions & Answers: Rio Marker Climate and Environment-Related Development Finance Statistics*, https://www.oecd.org/dac/financing-sustainable-development/development-finance-standards/FAQ_Tracking%20climate%20finance%20and%20Rio%20markers_February%202
. [2]

OECD (n.d.), *DAC and CRS code lists*, https://www.oecd.org/dac/financing-sustainable-development/development-finance-standards/dacandcrscodelists.htm (accessed on 16 September 2022). [8]

OECD (n.d.), *DAC List of ODA Recipients*, https://www.oecd.org/dac/financing-sustainable-development/development-finance-standards/daclist.htm (accessed on 31 October 2023). [16]

OECD (n.d.), *OECD DAC Rio Markers for Climate: Handbook*, https://www.oecd.org/dac/environment-development/Revised%20climate%20marker%20handbook_FINAL.pdf. [5]

TOSSD (2024), *TOSSD Reporting Instructions*, https://tossd.org/docs/2024_Reporting_Instructions.pdf (accessed on 24 June 2024). [13]

TOSSD (2024), *Total Official Support for Sustainable Development*, https://www.tossd.org/. [12]

Note

[1] Yet, reporting on the SDG focus in the TOSSD is a mandatory field.

Annex B. Sector classifications

Purpose codes

In the *Creditor Reporting System* (CRS), data on the sector of finance destination are recorded using purpose codes (OECD, n.d.[1]), reflecting the specific area of the recipient's economic or social structure that the transfer is intended to foster. Some contributions are not susceptible to allocation by sector and are reported as non-sector allocable aid. For this analysis, as seen in Table A B.1. , some purpose codes were reclassified into sector areas, seeking to depict activities captured through purpose codes within sector areas that are related by descriptions or functions.

Table A B.1. Purpose codes classified by sector areas

Sector areas	Purpose codes descriptions
Agriculture	Agricultural policy and administrative management, Agricultural development, Agricultural land resources, Agricultural water resources, Agricultural inputs, Food crop production, Industrial crops/export crops, Livestock, Agrarian reform, Agricultural alternative development, Agricultural extension, Agricultural education/training, Agricultural research, Agricultural services, Plant and post-harvest protection and pest control, Agricultural financial services, Agricultural co-operatives, Livestock/veterinary services
Education	Education policy and administrative management, Education facilities and training, Teacher training, Educational research, Primary education, Basic life skills for adults, Basic life skills for youth, Primary education equivalent for adults, Early childhood education, School feeding, Lower secondary education, Upper Secondary Education (modified and includes data from 11322), Vocational training, Higher education, Advanced technical and managerial training
Energy	Energy policy and administrative management, Energy sector policy, planning and administration, Energy regulation, Energy education/training, Energy research, Energy conservation and demand-side efficiency, Energy generation, renewable sources - multiple technologies, Hydro-electric power plants, Solar energy for centralised grids, Solar energy for isolated grids and standalone systems, Solar energy - thermal applications, Wind energy, Marine energy, Geothermal energy, Biofuelfired power plants, Energy generation, non-renewable sources, unspecified, Coal-fired electric power plants, Oil-fired electric power plants, Natural gas-fired electric power plants, Fossil fuel electric power plants with carbon capture and storage (CCS), Non-renewable waste-fired electric power plants, Hybrid energy electric power plants, Nuclear energy electric power plants and nuclear safety, Heat plants, District heating and cooling, Electric power transmission and distribution (centralised grids), Electric power transmission and distribution (isolated mini-grids), Retail gas distribution, Retail distribution of liquid or solid fossil fuels, Electric mobility infrastructures
Disaster Risk Reduction	Disaster Risk Reduction, Material relief assistance and services, Basic Health Care Services in Emergencies, Education in emergencies, Emergency food assistance, Relief co-ordination and support services, Immediate post-emergency reconstruction and rehabilitation, Multi-hazard response preparedness
Financial Systems[1]	Financial policy and administrative management, Monetary institutions, Formal sector financial intermediaries, Informal/semiformal financial intermediaries, Remittance facilitation, promotion and optimisation, Education/training in banking and financial services
Fishing	Fishing policy and administrative management, Fishery development, Fishery education/training, Fishery research, Fishery services
Forestry	Forestry policy and administrative management, Forestry development, Fuelwood/charcoal, Forestry education/training, Forestry research, Forestry services
General Environment Protection	Environmental policy and administrative management, Biosphere protection, Biodiversity, Site preservation, Environmental education/training, Environmental research
Government, Policies and Regulations	Public sector policy and administrative management, Public finance management (PFM), Decentralisation and support to subnational government, Anti-corruption organisations and institutions, Domestic revenue mobilisation, Tax collection, Budget planning, National audit, Debt and aid management, Foreign affairs, Diplomatic missions, Administration of developing countries' foreign aid, General personnel services, Public Procurement, Other general public services, National monitoring and evaluation, Local government finance, Other central transfers to institutions, Legal and judicial development, Justice, law and order policy, planning and administration, Police, Fire and rescue services, Judicial affairs,

Sector areas	Purpose codes descriptions
	Ombudsman, Immigration, Prisons, Macroeconomic policy, Meteorological services, National standards development, Democratic participation and civil society, Elections, Legislatures and political parties, Media and free flow of information, Executive office, Tax policy and administration support, Other non-tax revenue mobilisation, Human rights, Women's rights organisations and movements, and government institutions, Ending violence against women and girls, Local government administration, Facilitation of orderly, safe, regular and responsible migration and mobility, Government and civil society statistics and data, Security system management and reform, Civilian peace-building, conflict prevention and resolution, Participation in international peacekeeping operations, Reintegration and SALW control, Removal of land mines and explosive remnants of war, Child soldiers (prevention and demobilisation), Business policy and administration, Privatisation, Business development services, Responsible business conduct, Trade policy and administrative management, Trade facilitation, Regional trade agreements (RTAs), Multilateral trade negotiations, Trade-related adjustment, Trade education/training
Health	Health policy and administrative management, Medical education/training, Medical research, Medical services, Health statistics and data, Basic health care, Basic health infrastructure, Basic nutrition, Infectious disease control, Health education, Malaria control, Tuberculosis control, COVID-19 control, Health personnel development, NCDs control, general, Tobacco use control, Control of harmful use of alcohol and drugs, Promotion of mental health and well-being , Other prevention and treatment of NCDs, Research for prevention and control of NCDs, Population policy and administrative management, Reproductive health care, Family planning, STD control including HIV/AIDS, Personnel development for population and reproductive health, Population statistics and data
Industry	Industrial policy and administrative management, Industrial development, Small and medium-sized enterprises (SME) development, Cottage industries and handicraft, Agro-industries, Forest industries, Textiles, leather and substitutes, Chemicals, Fertilizer plants, Cement/lime/plaster, Energy manufacturing (fossil fuels), Pharmaceutical production, Basic metal industries, Non-ferrous metal industries, Engineering, Transport equipment industry, Modern biofuels manufacturing, Clean cooking appliances manufacturing, Technological research and development
Mineral Resources and Mining	Mineral/mining policy and administrative management, Mineral prospection and exploration, Coal, Oil and gas (upstream), Ferrous metals, Nonferrous metals, Precious metals/materials, Industrial minerals, Fertilizer minerals, Offshore minerals
Other Economic Infrastructure	Transport policy and administrative management, Transport policy, planning and administration, Public transport services, Transport regulation, Road transport, Feeder road construction, Feeder road maintenance, National road construction, National road maintenance, Rail transport, Water transport, Air transport, Storage, Education and training in transport and storage, Communications policy and administrative management, Communications policy, planning and administration, Postal services, Information services, Telecommunications, Radio/television/print media, Information and communication technology (ICT), Construction policy and administrative management
Other Multisector	Multisector aid, Urban development and management, Urban land policy and management, Urban development, Rural development, Rural land policy and management, Rural development, Non-agricultural alternative development, Food security policy and administrative management, Household food security programmes, Food safety and quality, Multisector education/training, Research/scientific institutions
Other Social Infrastructure and Services	Social Protection, Social protection and welfare services policy, planning and administration, Social security (excl. pensions), General pensions, Civil service pensions, Social services (incl. youth development and women+ children), Employment creation, Housing policy and administrative management, Low-cost housing, Multisector aid for basic social services, Culture and recreation, Statistical capacity building, Narcotics control, Social mitigation of HIV/AIDS, Recreation and sport, Culture, Labour rights, Social dialogue
Tourism	Tourism policy and administrative management
Unallocated / Unspecified	General budget support-related aid, Food assistance, Import support (capital goods), Import support (commodities), Action relating to debt, Debt forgiveness, Relief of multilateral debt, Rescheduling and refinancing, Debt for development swap, Other debt swap, Debt buy-back, Administrative costs (non-sector allocable), Refugees/asylum seekers in donor countries (non-sector allocable), Refugees/asylum seekers in donor countries - training, Refugees/asylum seekers in donor countries - rescue at sea, Sectors not specified, Promotion of development awareness (non-sector allocable), NULL
Water Supply and Sanitation	Water sector policy and administrative management, Water resources conservation (including data collection), Water supply and sanitation - large systems, Water supply - large systems, Sanitation - large systems, Basic drinking water supply and basic sanitation, Basic drinking water supply, Basic sanitation, River basins development, Waste management/disposal, Education and training in water supply and sanitation

1. Financial-related systems corresponding to the agriculture socio-economic sector are included in agriculture.
Notes: Sector areas were classified according to the CRS guidelines and further consulted with internal and external experts. This list of sector areas has been elaborated by the authors for the purpose of this analysis.

Thematic analysis

Additional methodologies for tracking ODF spending and activities that are related to biodiversity have been included in previous reports (OECD, 2023[2]), namely to identify whether activities supported marine or terrestrial biodiversity; ecosystem-based adaptation and ecosystem-based mitigation; illegal wildlife trade; capacity development; and Indigenous peoples and local communities (IPs and LCs). In particular, this report has updated the methodology on IPs and LCs. The following section provides details on the approach used.

Indigenous peoples and local communities

The methodology chosen to depict ODF targeting IPs and LCs builds upon a keyword search (Table A B.2.) based on insights found within the OECD-DAC CRS as well as building on past work, namely on *A Decade of Biodiversity Development Finance* (OECD, 2023[2]). This approach is applied to 2022 bilateral DAC members' activities captured as biodiversity-related (e.g. through the biodiversity Rio marker and SDGs 14 and 15). In addition, the methodology includes an additional layer of granularity by classifying a sample of activities into categories based on a range of examples found in Path to Scale (2024[3]); GATC (2023[4]), FTFG (2022[5]), Forest Peoples Programme (2022[6]), UNDP (2022[7]), WWF et al. (2021[8]), IPBES (2019[9]), Oviedo and Kenza Ali (2018[10]), GIZ (2016[11]), and GEF (2008[12]), as well as looking into the CRS (OECD DAC CRS, 2024[13]). While not exhaustive, the classification aims to provide a better understanding of biodiversity-related ODF that is related to, and includes, IPs and LCs considerations. Indeed, identifying these activities within the CRS can be challenging (e.g. it provides information on the first implementing partner) and more information would be needed to provide more accurate conclusions (e.g. technical notes, consultations, monitoring and evaluation reports, etc). Ultimately, the methodology seeks to improve the understanding of environmental activities that are related to, and can include, IPs and LCs.

Table A B.2. Indigenous peoples and local communities related keywords

Development and biodiversity context

Language	Keywords
English	aboriginal, aboriginal controlled, adat communities, agroforesters, agropastoralists, amplify Indigenous voices, ancestral, ancestral domain, ancestral land, ancestral memory, ancestral territories, ancestral uses, animal-human-animal, Artisanal, Artisanal and Small Scale Gold Mining, Biocultural Heritage Territory, Certified indigenous, chiefdoms, clan, CLLD, coastal communities, coastal fishing communities, co-designed with communities, coexistence of people and wildlife, collective rights, Collective titling, co-management regimes, communal land, communal land claims, communal ownership, communal protected areas, communally owned, communities self-determination and land rights, community assemblies, community conservation, community conserved, community conserved areas, community enterprises, community forest, community forest management, community forestry enterprises, community gardens, community lands, community nursery seedling capacity, community participation, Community Partnership, community rights, community rights to land, community-based biodiversity conservation, community-based coastal resource management, community-based conservation, community-based coral restoration, community-based forest enterprises, community-based management and governance, community-based natural resource management, community-based tree nurseries, community-centred conservation, community-

Language	Keywords
	conserved areas, community-led approach, Community-led conservation, community-led eco-tourism, Community-led nature-based solutions, community-led nature-based technologies, community-level support for gibbon conservation, community-managed, community-managed small loan, community-owned land, community-public-private partnerships, councils of elders, cultural and linguistic survival work, cultural rights, customary access, customary communities, customary governance, customary governance of wetlands, customary guardianship, customary institutions, customary land areas, customary land rights, customary practices, customary rights, customary sustainable use, customary tenure, customary use, customary-property-regime arrangements, custom-based systems, elders, empower communities, environmental defenders, environmental reconciliation, ethnic groups, ethnic people, ethnotourism, extractors, First Nations, fisher communities, fisher people, fisherfolk, fishermen, fishers, fishing communities , foragers, forest communities, forest dependent communities, forest peoples, forest rights, forest stewards, forest-based self-cultural identification, forest-dependent communities, forest-dependent populations, foresters, Formalizing Indigenous tenure, FPIC, Free, Prior and Informed Consent, gatherers, grassroots alliances, Guardians of life, guardians of the forests, herders, hill tribes, human-elephant, human-wildlife conflict, hunter-gatherer, hunters, ICCAs, ICCA Registry, IIFB, ILK, inclusive conservation, Indigenous Affairs, indigenous agricultural community, indigenous and traditional territories, Indigenous and Community Conserved Areas, indigenous and community land, indigenous and local knowledge, indigenous areas, indigenous community, indigenous communities, Indigenous councils, indigenous cultural, indigenous culture, indigenous descent, indigenous ecological knowledge, indigenous enterprises, indigenous ethnic groups, indigenous families, indigenous federations, indigenous forest community, indigenous funds, Indigenous governance, indigenous groups, Indigenous guardianship, indigenous issues, indigenous knowledge, indigenous land, indigenous landscapes, Indigenous Led Funds, indigenous Mayan communities, Indigenous national park staff members, Indigenous Partners, indigenous peasant territories, Indigenous People, indigenous people in voluntary isolation, Indigenous peoples, Indigenous Peoples-driven, indigenous population, Indigenous Program, Indigenous Protected Areas, indigenous rights, indigenous rural, indigenous territories, indigenous traditional knowledge, Indigenous voices, indigenous woman, indigenous women, Indigenous Women's Biodiversity Network, Indigenous women-led, Indigenous-controlled, indigenous-led, Indigenous-owned land, indigenous knowledge, indigenous and local languages, inter-generational leadership, International Indigenous Forum on Biodiversity, IPLC, IPLR , IPs and LCs, IP&LC, IP&LCs, IPs&LCs, isolated groups, IWBN, land grabbing, land rights, land tenure, land titling, land-connected peoples, land-sea people, LMMA, local and indigenous community enterprises, local communities, Local Communities and Indigenous Peoples, local community, local community action to conserve, local conservation committees, local conservation leadership, Local Ecological Knowledge, local ecotourism, local knowledge, local peoples, local resource users, local solutions, Locally Managed Marine Areas, migratory lifestyle, mining communities, mobile communities, Mother Earth centric actions, mountain communities, mountain societies, mountainous populations, Multiethnic Indigenous Territory, nature-dependent communities, nature's caregivers, nomadic lifestyle, nomadic tribes, non-indigenous traditional rural communities, OECMs, original inhabitants, Participatory Forest Management, participatory forest patrol, pastoral communities, pastoral people, Pastoralism, pastoralist, pastoralist communities, pastoralist land tenure security, pastoralist women, pastoralist women-led, paysans, peasant associations, peasant communities, peasant land, peasantry, pygmies, raft fishing communities, rights-based approach, rights-based conservation, rubber tappers, rural community, rural community tourism, rural indigenous population, rural pastoral, scheduled tribes, small farmers, small farming families, smallholder agriculture, small-scale farmers, social forestry, statutory and customary norms, stewards of nature, stewardship for sustainable management, strengthening tenure and resource rights, strengthening the rights of indigenous, subsistence farmers, subsistence farming, sustainable community forest management, tenure of collective titles, tenure security, tenure-related barriers, territorial attachment, territorial communities, territorial rights, territories and areas conserved by indigenous peoples and local communities, TICCA, titling demands, totems, Tradition with conservation, traditional authorities, traditional ceremony, traditional coastal communities, traditional communities, traditional ecological knowledge, traditional fisherfolk, traditional fisheries, traditional governance, Traditional hunting, traditional identity, traditional knowledge, traditional lands, traditional leaders, traditional methods, traditional occupations, traditional peoples, traditional practices, traditional rights, traditional riparian communities, traditional seeds, traditional territories, transmigrated community, tribal, tribal clans, tribal communities, tribal groups, tribal peoples, tribes, UNDRIP, United Nations Declaration on the Rights of Indigenous Peoples, UNPFII, village leaders, vital partners, water tenure
Spanish	(agro)pastorales, agricultura familiar, área comunal, área de conservación fluvial comunitaria, áreas indígenas protegidas, áreas marinas gestionadas localmente, autodeterminación de PPII, autoridades tradicionales, basados en la comunidad, bosques comunitarios, cohesión territorial indígena, comunidades amazónicas, comunidades campesinas, comunidades costeras, comunidades de bosque, comunidades étnicas, comunidades indígenas, comunidades locales, comunidades miskitas, comunidades pesqueras artesanales, comunidades rurales, comunidades rurales indígenas, conocimiento ancestral, conocimiento indígena, conocimiento local, conocimiento tradicional, conocimientos ancestrales, conocimientos indígenas, conocimientos locales, conocimientos tradicionales, conservación comunitaria, conservación de base comunitaria, custodios ambientales locales, custodios de sus tierras, custodios vitales, Defensores de la Naturaleza, derechos a las tierras, aguas y recursos, desarrollo comunitario, dirigidos por indígenas, distribución de beneficios a la comunidad, diversidad étnica, enfoque de conservación basado en los derechos, etnocidio, familias campesinas, Familias Lingüísticas Amazónicas, formas indígenas, formas tradicionales,

Language	Keywords
	gastronomía tradicional, gestión comunitaria, gestión forestal conjunta, gobernados por regímenes consuetudinarios, gobernanza comunitaria, gobernanza territorial indígena, guardianes ambientales, Guardianes de la vida, iniciativas basadas en la comunidad, instituciones pesqueras comunitarias, jóvenes indígenas, juventud indígena, leyes consuetudinarias, liderazgo indígena, líderes indígenas, lideresas y líderes comunitarios, los pueblos indígenas y las comunidades locales, mecanismos tradicionales, medicina tradicional, minorías étnicas, mujeres amazónicas, mujeres campesinas, Mujeres Campesinas Indígenas Originarias, mujeres indígenas, organización comunitaria, organizaciones de base comunitaria, organizaciones étnicas, organizaciones indígenas, organizaciones indígenas y campesinas, pesca artesanal, pescadores locales, pesquerías a pequeña escala, poblaciones indígenas y campesinas, prácticas agroecológicas tradicionales, prácticas campesinas tradicionales, productores de pequeña escala, productores tradicionales, pueblos indígenas, pueblos indoamericanos, quechuas, quilombolas, saberes tradicionales, sabios indígenas, sistema ancestral, sistema de tagal, sistemas alimentarios tradicionales, sistemas consuetudinarios de derechos, sistemas tradicionales de acuicultura, TerrIndigena, Territorio Multiétnico Indígena, territorios indígenas, textiles artesanales, Tierra Comunitaria, Tierra de los Ancestros, tierras ancestrales, tierras comunitarias, zona Indígena
French	Aborigènes, activités des communautés, association autochtone, autodétermination des peuples indigènes, capacités communautaires, chefs coutumiers, collectivités territoriales, communauté villageoise, communautés autochtones, communautés indigènes, communautés pastorales, communautés rurales, communautés villageoises, connaissances ancestrales, connaissances traditionnelles, Coopératives Agropastorales, couloir biologique intercommunautaire, élevage communautaire, enfants indigènes, exploitations agricoles de type familial, familles de pêcheurs, femmes agricultrices des villages, filières agropastorales, forêt communautaire, forêt-faune-populations, gardes forestiers, gestion communautaire, groupes autochtones, identité ethnique, indigènes , initiatives communautaires, initiatives de conservation communautaires, l'engagement des communautés autochtones et locales, mécanismes traditionnels, méthodes communautaires, modes de vie traditionnels, organisation autochtone, Participation des populations autochtones, peuples autochtone, peuples autochtones, PICL, plantes médicinales traditionnelles, pratiques ancestrales, régimes de propriété communautaire des ressources, réserve indienne, sagesse traditionnelles, sauvegarder les connaissances ancestrales, savoirs ancestraux, savoirs traditionnels, secteur minier artisanal, territoires autochtones, territoires indigènes, tribaux, tribus indigènes

Notes: This list is not exhaustive. Keywords are organised in alphabetical order and do not indicate any particular importance nor priority. Additional terms, such as "Indigenous Women's Biodiversity Network" or "Aboriginal and Torres Strait Islanders", could also have been included in this list but are captured through shorter keywords already mentioned (e.g. "Indigenous women" or "aboriginal").

Table A B.3. Classification of environmental activities related to Indigenous peoples and local communities

Development and biodiversity context

Classification	Scope	Activities examples	Theme by CRS examples (sector and purpose name)
Capacity building, technology transfer and knowledge exchange	Support to development and management of human and technological resources, as well as institution building, education, research, training and knowledge sharing, including: indigenous and local ecological knowledge, strengthening capacities, mutual learning and sharing	Creating an enabling environment and building governmental and non-governmental capacity to support community-based environmental protection initiatives, and transferring lessons learnt to other regions.	General Environment Protection (Environmental policy and administrative management)
		Creating multi-stakeholder knowledge platforms, enabling collaboration, learning and exchange.	Government and Civil Society (Democratic participation and civil society)
		Share technology and training to create scalable, nature-based conservation models for the world's most vital ecosystems.	General Environment Protection (Environmental education/training)
		Promote the sharing of traditional knowledge and experience. Setting up a socio-environmental information centre for indigenous territories.	Other Social Infrastructure and Services (Culture and cultural diversity)
		Technical knowledge and advice to strengthen local capacities in the mineral and mining sector.	Mineral Resources and Mining

Classification	Scope	Activities examples	Theme by CRS examples (sector and purpose name)
	platforms, and data collection and statistical activities.		(Mineral/mining policy and administrative management)
		Leverage technological and conceptual breakthroughs in environmental data collection, processing and communication to enhance resilience building in data-scarce and poor mountain communities.	General Environment Protection (Environmental research)
Conflict, peace and security	Peace building, conflict prevention, mitigation, management and resolution mechanisms, security and defense, including to address: illegal cross-border trade, forest/park encroachment, illegal logging, illegal wildlife trade, monitoring environmental crimes, patrol, threats, human-wildlife conflict.	Identify conflicts that may exist regarding the exercise of Indigenous and community rights to natural resources in relation to other stakeholders' entitlements and interests, and seek opportunities to facilitate negotiation and conflict resolution with third parties to secure the rights and needs of local communities.	Conflict, Peace and Security (Civilian peace-building, conflict prevention and resolution)
		Improve the chiefs/traditional authorities' ability to effectively combat threats from within and without by providing basic training for them which will allow them to understand the consequences of threats to the local communities, such as illegal surface mining, illegal chain saw operations, etc.	Conflict, Peace and Security (Civilian peace-building, conflict prevention and resolution)
		Assistance to local communities that facilitates orderly and responsible migration and mobility due to environmental projects resulting in forced displacement.	Government and Civil Society (Facilitation of orderly, safe, regular and responsible migration and mobility)
		Security, threats (e.g. communities defending their land from transition mineral mining projects are seeing an increased risk of threats and attacks).	Conflict, Peace and Security (Civilian peace-building, conflict prevention and resolution)
		Legal support to communities in conflict, including litigation and court cases, as well as support to environmental defenders.	Government and Civil Society (Legal and judicial development)
Energy	Energy sector policy and planning, regulation, renewable energy generation programmes, village grids and electricity storage and distribution technologies. For example, fuelwood/charcoal reduction programmes, support for alternative energy sources and energy efficient initiatives.	Support access to and use of alternative energy sources and capacity building on environmental conservation, contributing to enhancing afforestation and sustainable livelihoods.	Energy policy (energy policy and administrative management)
		Encourage the use of alternative energy to wood, support efficient biomass/firewood stoves, and scaling up renewable energy to reduce and replace the consumption of wood.	Forestry (Fuelwood/charcoal); Industry (Clean cooking appliances manufacturing)
		Develop an integrated watershed protection plan and implement watershed restoration measures, using micro-hydropower systems to incentivise the conservation of watersheds.	Energy generation, renewable sources (Hydro-electric power plants)
Environmental protection	Environmental and land use planning and decision making; conservation and protection measures, including natural reserves and actions in the surrounding areas and measures to protect endangered species and their	Support Indigenous peoples and local communities (IPs and LCs) to protect land, water, territories and biodiversity through a rights-based approach. Securing forest guardianship role of Indigenous peoples and forest dependent communities. Support the creation, expansion and management of protected and conserved areas globally.	General Environment Protection (Biodiversity)
		Community based landscape protection and rehabilitation of spring water catchment that serve to maintain humidity on the mountain as well as the whole catchment; community-based conservation to save biodiversity watershed.	General Environment Protection (Biodiversity)
		Consolidating territorial and environmental management in Indigenous lands, including through the	General Environment Protection

Classification	Scope	Activities examples	Theme by CRS examples (sector and purpose name)
	habitats. For example, co-management of protected areas, community-based conservation and restoration, community-led nature-based solutions, environmental justice, environmental stewardship, forest guardianship, Indigenous and community conserved areas, local conservation committees and leadership, monitoring and vigilance activities, monitoring deforestation, OECMs, participatory forest patrol, access and benefit sharing, reduce hunting pressures, conservation rights-based approach.	conservation and management of natural resources, and education for environmental management.	(Environmental policy and administrative management)
		Raising awareness among the local population in the surrounding area of critical ecosystems so that the importance of protecting these lands are understood, and so that local people may also contribute to maintaining a vigilant attitude towards the integrity of the natural resources present there, which are threatened by the activities taking place in the surrounding area.	General Environment Protection (Biodiversity)
		Monitor the impact and effectiveness of conservation areas established by customary landowners so as to inform and guide future work to strengthen and adapt traditional approaches to environmental protection.	General Environment Protection (Environmental policy and administrative management)
		Support for fieldwork, monitoring, surveillance, forest fire prevention and management. Train forest rangers to protect the area from illegal logging and poachers.	General Environment Protection (Biodiversity)
		Develop and pilot a mechanism of access and benefit sharing for sustainable collection of medicinal plants, contributing to biodiversity conservation and indigenous knowledge preservation for the wellbeing of forest dependent ethnic minorities.	General Environment Protection (Biodiversity)
		Ensure effective management of marine ecosystems to secure the long-term health of the ocean and the services it provides.	General Environment Protection (Environmental policy and administrative management)
Finance and business development	Support to business and investment environment, including: business development, financial market and regulations, property rights, customary property-regime arrangements, support to Indigenous-led funds and community enterprises, enabling commercial programmes, credit lines and matchmaking services, providing direct aid programmes and funding.	Facilitate direct, sustainable and efficient funding by establishing regional and national mechanisms, fostering capacity building, and facilitating dialogue between donors and partners.	Banking and Financial Services (Education/training in banking and financial services)
		Support capacity to access and manage official development assistance (ODA) and national funds.	Banking and Financial Services (Education/training in banking and financial services)
		Increase the capacity, skills and role of women artisans in product development (e.g. woven pandanus leaf crafts); the use of natural fibers and dyes; and organic vegetable attention to aspects of economic, ecological and socio-cultural (local knowledge) management, resulting in increased revenue, qualified products and in accordance with market demand.	Industry (Industrial policy and administrative management)
		Establish a sustainability financial strategy for the management of protected areas and biological corridors.	General Environment Protection (Environmental policy and administrative management)
		Strengthen value chains as a mechanism to facilitate the articulation between actors in a productive chain, within the framework of good environmental practices and under an equitable distribution of social and economic benefits among participants.	Agriculture (Agricultural financial services; Agricultural alternative development)
		Support the development of entrepreneurs of local resources through the sustainable and diversified use of biodiversity, with added value to their products, and the creation and strengthening of local, national and export markets that generate equity and economic and social well-being. This implies	Industry (Small and medium-sized enterprises (SME) development);

Classification	Scope	Activities examples	Theme by CRS examples (sector and purpose name)
		promoting the development of conditions that allow communities to assume themselves as decisive actors in the fate of the sustainable use of their natural capital and, consequently, as market agents, in order to change economic strategies towards profitable schemes.	
		Strengthen socio-economic sustainability (management, productive, financial and market management).	Industry (Small and medium-sized enterprises (SME) development)
		Strengthen property rights.	Business and Other Services (Business policy and administration)
Governance	Support to governance, management systems, co-ordination, planning and reform, democratic participation, engage and hold governments to account, improve civilian oversight. For example, ensuring Free, Prior and Informed Consent (FPIC); civic participation; projects co-designed with communities; community consultations and participation; conservation governance; strengthening constructive dialogue; institutionalisation of dialogue mechanisms; customary governance; decision making; inclusive reforms; intercultural communication; participatory land-use planning; shared agreements; social cohesion; trust mechanisms.	Support the establishment of more effective land governance systems strengthening participation and governance (e.g. adapting laws and policies to enable more and better participation), and generating spaces for territorial governance based on traditional and self-determination mechanisms.	Government and Civil Society (Democratic participation and civil society)
		Participation of indigenous and local communities in the design, implementation, management, monitoring and evaluation of funded projects.	Business and Other Services (Responsible business conduct)
		Explore options for promoting legal and policy reform to strengthen provisions for community participation.	Business and Other Services (Responsible business conduct)
		Promote constructive and direct dialogue with IP and LC leaders and representative organisations in land and forest tenure reform processes (e.g. Global Alliance of Territorial Communities), providing a better understanding of challenges faced by communities and showcasing proactive collaboration with IP and LC stakeholders.	Other Social Infrastructure and Services (Social dialogue)
		Co-management or direct participation of IPs and LCs of protected areas and buffer zones.	General Environment Protection (Biodiversity)
		Consultation and involvement of protected area sponsors and managers, project-affected communities, including indigenous peoples, and other stakeholders in the planning, design, implementation, monitoring and evaluation of the proposed project, as appropriate; reflect the concerns of potentially affected communities and other stakeholders.	General Environment Protection (Environmental policy and administrative management)
		Integrate national implementation strategies and action plans on sustainable development, biodiversity and climate change, based on inclusive participatory approaches and decentralised decision making.	General Environment Protection (Environmental policy and administrative management)
		Raise awareness and promote the participation of Indigenous peoples in the Convention on Biological Diversity and Global Environment Facility-related processes, establishing communication and information mechanisms that promote effective information exchange.	Government and Civil Society (Democratic participation and civil society)
		Include the participation of local communities in social, health and environmental programmes related to mineral extraction and processing.	Mineral Resources and Mining (Mineral/mining policy and administrative management)
Human rights	Support human rights, and promote and protect civil and political, economic, social and cultural rights, including to	Support for international advocacy and communications (e.g. on tenure security, biodiversity, and climate change), as well as creating spaces for Indigenous voices and ideas including by facilitating the participation in international negotiations and processes (e.g. the Convention on Biological Diversity).	Government and Civil Society (Human rights)

Classification	Scope	Activities examples	Theme by CRS examples (sector and purpose name)
	strengthen legislation, reporting, dialogue, human rights defenders and advocacy, awareness raising and non-discrimination including to: amplify Indigenous voices and representation; appropriate recognition and support, community empowerment; women's rights; customary rights; a human rights-based approach; judicial protection; local empowerment of action for development; protection from incursions, intimidation, and violence; reciprocity; traditional rights.	Promote human rights-based approaches to raise awareness and support rights-holders, such as IPs and LCs, to claim and realise their rights while simultaneously supporting state institutions to fulfill their obligations to respect, protect and fulfill human rights.	Government and Civil Society (Human rights)
		Strengthen awareness and transparency, enable reviews, reporting, media, alerting and research (e.g. on killings or attacks against human rights defenders).	Government and Civil Society (Media and free flow of information)
		Through rights-based approaches in conservation, like the right to information or the right to security and freedom from discrimination, promote equity and reconciliation in conservation initiatives.	Government and Civil Society (Human rights)
		Strengthen policy and the legal environment conducive for security of environmental human rights defenders, and protect Indigenous and community defenders of forests and nature.	Government and Civil Society (Human rights)
		Strengthen effective safeguards that ensure that human rights are not violated, including of environmental defenders, in the implementation of sustainable development and biodiversity and climate change measures.	Business and Other Services (Responsible business conduct)
		Promote the principle of free, prior and informed consent in mining activities, ensuring that indigenous and local community voices are considered.	Mineral Resources and Mining (Mineral/mining policy and administrative management)
		Provide legal protection in the face of ongoing threats, intimidation, criminalisation and violence.	Government and Civil Society (Legal and judicial development)
Land and water tenure and resources rights	Land use planning and decision making procedures, land reclamation and reforms, tenure access and rights. For example, access, control, use and ownership of lands, forests and water, cadastral systems and participatory mapping, land registration and recognition, land titling, land use reform, communal land claims, customary land rights, forest tenure reform, formalizing Indigenous tenure, Indigenous peoples land rights, resource rights, strengthening tenure security, territorial rights.	Support to map, document, develop cadastral systems and register lands, including support to community-level tenure rights mapping and registration work.	Agriculture (Agricultural land resources)
		Assert or claim legal rights to land, forests and water (formal rights recognition), ensuring there is recognition of natural resources rights in new laws and that reform processes include communities.	General Environment Protection (Environmental policy and administrative management)
		Support comprehensive reforms to improve equitable access to land and tenure security, and provide clarity on land tenure, use and access to natural resources and knowledge.	Agriculture (Agricultural land resources)
		Measures to ensure customary land tenure or systems of communal property of resources, and defend their rights.	Agriculture (Agricultural land resources)
		Measures to ensure customary water tenure and defend their rights.	Water Supply and Sanitation (Water sector policy and administrative management)
		Support comprehensive reforms to improve equitable access to land and tenure security.	Agriculture (Agricultural policy and administrative management)
		Protect critical local watershed through sound land management, awareness and institutional support to the existing local communities, e.g. through water resources protection awareness, fencing around landslide areas, plantation on landslide areas.	Water Supply and Sanitation (Water resources conservation)
Partnerships	Support alliances and network building of international and local organisations, movements	Promote a network of indigenous communities to preserve biodiversity and promote sustainable and culturally acceptable land use.	General Environment Protection (Environmental policy and administrative management)

Classification	Scope	Activities examples	Theme by CRS examples (sector and purpose name)
	and institutions to enhance their effectiveness, influence, facilitate exchange, build trust and increase collaborations across stakeholders. For example, by fostering community partnerships, community-public-private partnerships, grassroots alliances, and facilitating dialogue.	Enhance partnerships between Indigenous peoples, government and private actors.	Business and Other Services (Business policy and administration)
		Build trust-based networks of people to collaborate for conservation.	General Environment Protection (Biodiversity)
		Support IPs- and LCs-led organisations and/or networks.	Government and Civil Society (Human rights)
Policies and institutions	Support to institutions and policy development; formulation of policies, laws and regulations; maintenance of law and order and public safety; law enforcement, legal aid and counsel; traditional, Indigenous and paralegal practices. For example, adequate regulatory and/or intercultural frameworks, customary institutions, forest laws, international policies, institutional arrangements, legal empowerment, local community protocols, statutory and customary norms.	Support the elaboration of public policies, as well as the harmonisation of relevant aspects of international and national law and policy.	Government and Civil Society (Legal and judicial development)
		Support strengthening and development of institutions and organisational capacities involving indigenous and local groups.	Government and Civil Society (Public sector policy and administrative management)
		Institutional and policy development.	Government and Civil Society (Public sector policy and administrative management)
Sustainable income and livelihoods	Employment creation and income generation programmes, sustainable economic opportunities, promotion of sustainable livelihoods and well-being, and food security and sovereignty.	Diversify income and generate alternative income through the development of ecologically intensive rice-growing and market gardening techniques.	Agriculture (Agricultural development)
		Support the development of alternative income-generating activities and sources of livelihoods, e.g. from innovations and diversification processes, and economic development.	Other Social Infrastructure and Services (Social protection and welfare services policy, planning and administration; and Employment creation)
		Inclusive economic development through the adoption of practices that integrate conservation needs and development priorities.	General Environment Protection (Environmental policy and administrative management)
		Promote food security through engaging with rural inhabitants and local communities, and other actors, in the preservation of biodiversity, forest management and sustainable production, with a keen focus	Other Multisector (Food security policy and administrative management)

Classification	Scope	Activities examples	Theme by CRS examples (sector and purpose name)
		on food and cash crops.	
		Planting of economically valued trees and plant-like fruit trees in strategic areas to generate income through, for example, selling fruits, timber and other forest products like fodders and broom grass, uplifting economic opportunities of community members.	Forestry (Forestry development)
Sustainable use and management of natural resources	Planning and development of nature-dependent economic activities (e.g. agriculture, forestry, fishing, mining, ecotourism), including: co-management regimes, community-based forest and coastal management and governance, eco-cultural tourism, integrated water/coastal/marine ecosystem management, transboundary management, responsible stewardship activities, traditional hunting, agroecology.	Systematic consideration of biodiversity in production areas through activities such as the promotion of sound agricultural practices based on the traditional knowledge of Indigenous communities.	Agriculture (Agricultural development)
		Strengthen cultural practices and methods for the sustainable management and use of natural resources and soil.	Agriculture (Agricultural land resources)
		Revitalise traditional practices, such as traditional aquaculture systems.	Fishing (Fishery development)
		Work with small-scale fisheries and aquaculture areas managed by local communities to implement socially responsible and sustainable harvesting practices.	Fishing (Fishery development)
		Support for sustainable forest management or other forest- or nature-based livelihood strategies.	Forestry (Forestry development)
		Support community-based ecotourism, including the promotion of ecotourism products, enhance eco/ethnotourism activities in the forest.	Tourism (Tourism policy and administrative management)
		Sustainable management of international waters.	Water Supply and Sanitation (Water resources conservation)

Notes: This table showcases a sample of possible activities funded with development finance and is designed for illustration purposes (the order of activities listed does not reflect a prioritisation of objectives). The "Theme by CRS examples" reflects possible categorisations of the activities based on the OECD-DAC CRS sector and purpose codes and definitions found in OECD (n.d.[14]).

References

Conway, J. and A. Medri (2022), "Las comunidades locales son clave para la conservación", https://stories.undp.org/comunidades-locales-clave-para-la-conservacion (accessed on 1 July 2024). [7]

Forest Peoples Programme (2022), *Perspectivas Locales sobre la Diversidad Biológica 2*, Forest Peoples Programme, Moreton-in-Marsh, United Kingdom, https://www.cbd.int/gbo/gbo5/publication/lbo-2-summary-es.pdf (accessed on 3 July 2024). [6]

FTFG (2022), *Indigenous Peoples and Local Communities Forest Tenure Pledge: Annual Report 2021-2022*, Forest Tenure Funders Group, https://www.fordfoundation.org/wp-content/uploads/2022/11/indigenous-peoples-and-local-communities-forest-tenure-pledge-annual-report-2021-2022.pdf (accessed on 5 July 2024). [5]

GATC (2023), "Shandia", web page, https://globalalliance.me/shandia (accessed on 25 July 2024). [4]

GEF (2008), *Communautés autochtones et biodiversité*, https://www.thegef.org/sites/default/files/publications/Indigenous-People-French-PDF.pdf (accessed on 1 July 2024). [12]

GIZ (2016), *Gobernanza de la Biodiversidad*, Deutsche Gesellschaft für Internationale Zusammenarbeit GmbH, https://www.giz.de/de/downloads/giz2016-es-Gobernanza_de_la_biodiversidad.pdf (accessed on 17 June 2024). [11]

IPBES (2019), *Global Assessment Report on Biodiversity and Ecosystem Services of the Intergovernmental Science-Policy Platform on Biodiversity and Ecosystem Services*, Intergovernmental Science-Policy Platform on Biodiversity and Ecosystem Services, Bonn, Germany, https://doi.org/10.5281/zenodo.3831673. [9]

OECD (2023), *A Decade of Development Finance for Biodiversity*, OECD Publishing, Paris, https://doi.org/10.1787/e6c182aa-en. [2]

OECD (n.d.), *DAC and CRS code lists*, https://www.oecd.org/dac/financing-sustainable-development/development-finance-standards/dacandcrscodelists.htm (accessed on 16 September 2022). [14]

OECD (n.d.), *Purpose Codes: sector classification*, https://www.oecd.org/development/financing-sustainable-development/development-finance-standards/purposecodessectorclassification.htm. [1]

OECD DAC CRS (2024), *OECD Data Explorer*, https://data-explorer.oecd.org/. [13]

Oviedo, G. and M. Kenza Ali (2018), *The Relationship of Indigenous Peoples and Local Communities with Wetlands*, Ramsar Convention Secretariat, https://www.ramsar.org/sites/default/files/documents/library/indigenous_peoples_local_communities_wetlands_e.pdf (accessed on 15 July 2024). [10]

Path to Scale (2024), *Path to Scale Funding Dashboard*, https://dashboard.pathtoscale.org (accessed on 16 July 2024). [3]

WWF et al. (2021), *The State of Indigenous Peoples' and Local Communities' Lands and Territories*, WWF, Gland, Switzerland, https://wwflac.awsassets.panda.org/downloads/report_the_state_of_the_indigenous_peoples_and_local_communities_lands_and_territories_1.pdf (accessed on 1 July 2024). [8]

www.ingramcontent.com/pod-product-compliance
Ingram Content Group UK Ltd.
Pitfield, Milton Keynes, MK11 3LW, UK
UKHW051507290926
15471UKWH00008B/1474

9 789264 437883